MW01204468

BOLSTER UP!

THE ULTIMATE GUIDE TO BECOMING A
HAPPY, HEALTHY
HUMAN

BOLSTER
UP!

STEPHANIE BOLSTER McCANNON

Bolster UP!

Copyright 2022 © Stephanie Bolster McCannon

All information, techniques, ideas and concepts contained within this publication are of the nature of general comment only and are not in any way recommended as individual advice. The intent is to offer a variety of information to provide a wider range of choices now and in the future, recognizing that we all have widely diverse circumstances and viewpoints. Should any reader choose to make use of the information contained herein, this is their decision, and the contributors (and their companies), authors and publishers do not assume any responsibilities whatsoever under any condition or circumstances. It is recommended that the reader obtain their own independent advice.

First Edition 2022

ISBN: 9798781452446

All rights reserved in all media. No part of this book may be used, copied, reproduced, presented, stored, communicated or transmitted in any form by any means without prior written permission, except in the case of brief quotations embodied in critical articles and reviews.

The moral right of Stephanie Bolster McCannon as the author of this work has been asserted by him in accordance with the Copyrights, Designs and Patents Act of 1988.

Published by Happy Self Publishing
www.happyselfpublishing.com
writetous@happyselfpublishing.com

HAPPY
SELF PUBLISHING

DEDICATION

I dedicate this book to all those suffering needlessly with health concerns, stress, and lack of work/life rhythm. You can have a more satisfying life, full of health, happiness, and enjoy being human!

APPRECIATION

I would like to thank Chase C McCannon for his ability and willingness to discuss the nuances of life with me.

Sara-Grace McCannon and Charlotte McCannon, thank you both for supporting me and encouraging me to follow my own dreams. Gail Casazza, for your amazing friendship, and Christopher Millard, for your unwavering belief in me and my "crazy" ideas.

WHAT OTHERS ARE SAYING

I just want to thank you personally for all your excellent guidance which has truly helped improve my health. You are an outstanding professional and your efforts have changed my perceptions about the value of health coaches.

I will always be grateful for your interest and coaching. A better gift, I could never have received.

Best always to you. I'll always remember you when I practice my breathing exercises!

– Tim, CEO

First, thank you so much for your energetic presentation at the Organizational Effectiveness meeting. You were one of the best guest speakers we have had!

– Beth

OMG!!! My staff absolutely LOVED Stephanie, loved her. She was passionate, motivated, energetic, simply wonderful. We are going to talk about bringing her back to another OE meeting, for longer than an hour, very soon!

– MedStar

Even though I've only worked with Stephanie a short time it has been a life-changing experience. I have attempted many healing modalities, and this one-by far-works the fastest. Stephanie has quickly helped me to reach new heights with my personal goals. Stephanie was able to pinpoint the cause of my issues, and then noticeably and quickly clear away the resistance that was hindering me from accomplishing my hopes and dreams. Stephanie is the perfect option for anyone who has felt stuck with their life and wants to quickly and painlessly remedy that to move forward.

– Vanessa

I want to give a huge shout out to Stephanie McCannon for delivering yet another very successful seminar for one of our customers. We had a provider call out sick at the end of the day Tuesday and Stephanie jumped in and offered to deliver the training on Wednesday morning! This was one of the best classes ever. Stephanie McCannon - you are amazing. Thank you!!!

– Dan

TABLE OF CONTENTS

FOREWORD

*B*olsterUp, *The Ultimate Guide to Becoming a Happy Healthy Human* is a wonderful mix of practical and easy to implement principles that you can follow to improve your overall wellbeing. Stephanie and I have several things in common. We both started our careers teaching students in inner-city schools how to rise above their circumstances and create lives of success. We both eventually had a vision of serving even more people outside of the classroom and around the world with the same unwavering belief in their potential and the powerful, practical principles and tools we had learned and successfully used. We both became successful coaches.

After achieving such great results time after time with her clients, Stephanie was then encouraged to write it all down and share her blueprints for attaining wellbeing. In *BolsterUp*, Stephanie has taken what are often experienced as the complexities of neuroscience, psychology, and sociology and broken them down into the 4 Pillars of wellbeing: Thinking, Breathing, Nourishment, and Rest. She shows you how to use each of these to greater health and happiness. In her successful integration of both science and heart, she shows you the impact small, simple, but powerful changes in your daily life can have on your experience of your health, relationships, career, and life.

Stephanie's focus on the health and wellness field started when she was a young mother and was diagnosed with an autoimmune disorder. Looking for ways to encourage her own body's health, she discovered the 4 principles all of us can use to support our mental, physical, and emotional health. She then continued her learning by becoming one of the first people to obtain certification as a Health and Wellness coach by Wellcoaches©, the same course that is now used at Harvard.

As a result of her highly successful practice, which includes working with a wide range of clients from Fortune 500 CEO's, physicians, lawyers, and teachers to factory workers and students, her work and reputation as a coach have been broadly recognized in the United States and around the world. And now in this book, Stephanie has chosen to bring this holistic approach to wellbeing, health and happiness to the masses.

I encourage you to read this book in its entirety. Underline in it and take notes. When you do, you will come away with the understanding of how and why your thinking, breathing, nourishment, and rest impacts your life...and what you can do about it starting now. More importantly, make the commitment to put Stephanie's hard-earned wisdom and sage advice into practice in your life. If you do, you can look forward to experiencing much greater health, happiness and wellbeing. And that is your birthright. It's now time to claim it!

I wish you well!

Jack Canfield, Co-author of the
Chicken Soup for the Soul® series and
The Success Principles™ and
How to Get from Where You Are to Where You Want to Be

FREE BONUS

I am on a mission to improve your life as safely, quickly and freely as possible to bolster-up your health, happiness and humanity.

Yes, you can GREATLY improve your stress, reverse burnout and turn the table on anxiety. With this short but effective and absolutely necessary 7 day challenge you will learn to use your breathing organs to find relief, peace and yes even some happiness!

I am going to TEACH you in 7 DAYS how to breath properly, AND provide 7 deliberate, and specific breathing techniques that:

- Increase energy and decrease exhaustion
- Increase mental alertness and positivity
- Decrease inflammation, weight gain, and blood pressure

Join me and the thousands of others who have benefited from this method already.

Take back your health, happiness and humanity with the BolsterUp Breathing challenge…7 Breaths of Peace.

Download Free Bonus

BolsterUpBonus

https://bit.ly/bolsterup

INTRODUCTION

> *"I don't give because I am happy.*
> *I am happy because I give."*
> - Stephanie McCannon

I am a *giver*. Whenever I buy someone a gift, I struggle impatiently until the "designated time" to give it to them. (Holidays and birthdays are torture!) I just can't wait to give. I love everything about it. Part of that love includes passing along information, knowledge, and understanding to others. So, it's no wonder I ended up becoming a teacher and coach. Over the years, I've found that when I give, I also get something, learn something new, and then immediately want to share it and give it away to others. It's an endless cycle, and my favorite part of what I do.

So, this book is my gift to you. In the pages that follow, I am (eagerly!) giving away the same great insights my clients have benefited from for years. Working with people worldwide has taught me that no matter our culture or continent, we all want the same thing from life: to feel good. But there is a sabotaging trickster who holds us back from the health, happiness, and the humanity we desire — ourselves. I'm here to help alleviate this disconnect within you and jumpstart your current reality to reflect more of what you want. Right here, right now.

But to start, you must know what you want, just choose it. Accept what it is like right now compared to what you want. No, actually, not just accept. You must be *thankful* for what is now — but eager for more! This is the great mystery: How do you find appreciation for the present while still working toward the future you want? The good news is that the solution is simple, surprisingly easy, and available to you now! You just have to be willing to set some structure and put a few systems in place. I can't wait to give you this gift. And if you want more gifts to unwrap, check out my online in depth video program at: www. theBolsterUpMethod.com.

CHAPTER 1

HOW DO
WE PERCEIVE MIND?

"The greatest discovery of any generation is that a human can alter his life by altering his attitude."
- William James

The power and products of intention to improve lifestyle involve psychology and physiology... mental and physical are always connected! Always. Thoughts become things... we truly do make something out of nothing!

Cognitive Behavior Theory states: thoughts, feelings, and behavior are the cycle of our interactions, moods, and resulting quality of life. I apply this psychotherapy premise along with the Process Healing Method, a rapid and efficient means to problem-solve and treat behaviors based on anxiety, fear, sadness, and other painful memories.[1]

---

[1] Flint, 2006, A Theory and Treatment of Your Personality.

In addition, advances in applied psychology and neuroscience have begun to show us the fascinating ability we all have to change our current reality. Our brains, and therefore thoughts, feelings, and behaviors are all malleable. I will share some of the science with you, as well as how to apply the knowledge I provide, in improving your own experience.

I love science and use both a Newtonian and Quantum thinking world view. Traditional Newtonian thinking may be called "mechanistic". It is based in reductionism, determinism, materialism, and a reflection-correspondence view of knowledge. Although it is simple, coherent and intuitive, it ignores or denies human agency, values, creativity and evolution. Where Newtonian thinking ends, quantum thinking begins. I merge both, and believe this is the best use of all thought knowledge we have available. Quantum thinking is the ability of the mind to view a problem from all sides and that includes Newtonian logic.

I have had many great, fascinating, and wise teachers in my life, and continue to expose myself to current ideas. Abraham Maslow, Fritz Perls, Carl Rogers, and Virginia Satie are among those that have shed light on the mental and physical connection, and how it is our choosing of the life we live, good or bad.

My first introduction to self-actualization was as a freshman in high school. I was drawn into the understanding of Maslow's Hierarchy of Needs, and to me, the promised success by emphasizing possibility, NOT pathology. It was an awakening that I had more control over the outcome in my life and it gave me permission to think outside my current circumstance. I did not have to live a victim's life. Maslow saw and offered that, our suffering (and mine was great) serves to bring out greater strengths. Woohoo! I was ready for the greater things for sure. I know you are too.

I awakened, shot out of my "woe is me" dream state, fully aware and alive by the hope of the strength I must have due to "my great suffering." I was electrified with happiness, overjoyed as a young teenage girl alone in my room that I could have a future. That I, a nobody, a poor girl kicked out of schools, quick to throw the first punch, last to have the final word, could be someone, something better! This was the sweetest music, which I was ready to play, although not knowing the notes, or understanding the instrument just yet. My lifelong journey of self- improvement had begun.

The shift many are making in the health care field, business, education, marketing, and more is the shift to focus on what is working. The process of changing behavior is complex, but I'm going to break it down into fun, manageable steps that feel good, are simple to implement, and most of all, are there for the taking.

MY COACH APPROACH

> *"To change one's life: 1. Start immediately.*
> *2. Do it flamboyantly.*
> *3. No exceptions. "*
> - William James

My profession, in its simplest form, is that of a coach. Coaching on health and well-being to some, on living a more fulfilling life to others. Most do not make the distinction. Unlike other helpful services, like counseling and seeing your physician, coaching takes a different approach by walking along-side the participant.

My work dictates that I listen, helping to uncover motivations and strengths, assist in implementing change. The goal is a lifestyle that is not only good for you, but feels good to you... your ideas are brought to life, and carefully, artfully implemented to create the behaviors and lifestyle so many are after... happy, healthy, and human.

Many will consider this book to be in the personal development genre. I am okay with that. With one caveat. My deviation from the mass of personal development dicta — and it is huge! Ready for it? — *There is nothing wrong with you*! You may benefit from thinking and lifestyle adjustments (structures), but fundamentally you are fine, better than fine...you're alright! It's all okay.

Whatever your struggles today, or what you may find in your current situation that you "don't want" … it is okay. You've reached this point somehow, and you can reach a better point… any choice you want, "somehow".

I know right now, you may want to throw this book against the wall, or in the trash, but stay with me. The truth is that most people just do not take action on the next step. Whether that step is calling a coach like me, putting on sneakers and going for a walk or jog, or just taking a very much needed deep breath to start a new chain of thought.

We sabotage ourselves for several reasons, which if you continue reading I'll outline. The goal within our grasp however, is accepting that you already are at a state of well-being. Appreciate your current circumstance. Continue to be open to moving towards *more,* towards the recognition that you are a happy, healthy human.

What I provide is a basic map, or the blueprint, to navigate the waters of a happy and healthy human life. Without the right map, or a good guide, you're not going to get where you want to go. It is important to know where you want to go *and* identify where you are right now. It's alright if you feel like there is so much wrong with you, or life, or even if it seems nothing goes your way. Just being willing to identify some of those feelings clues you in to where you are. However, it is important to take another look around, to see what is going well. *BolsterUP* is your guide, the map to help you find your fountain of youth, treasures in life, and overall abundance. I cover much more in detail in the online video course @TheBolsterUpMethod.com.

I am going to help you discover your peace and place. To create a newer and better feeling of health and happiness. Just stay with me until the end. I promise there is hope and more clarity in your journey towards the happy, healthy human life we all seek.

THE EARLY DAYS

Way back in my early teaching days, I was in charge of a rambunctious, eager to make a mess, preschool class. I had a rare opportunity to teach a valuable lifelong lesson, or so I thought. One of my darlings, who was just learning how to count, and keep glue out of "the things I can eat category", had a propensity for hitting.

Many of the other eager crayon eaters often chose a dinosaur out of the toy collection to play with. My Mike Tyson in the making, quite often also wanted that same dinosaur. With a wind up he'd hit whoever had it seeking a quick release to satisfy his selfish pleasure.

Of course this behavior was unacceptable. So was the way it was frequently dealt with by the other teachers. I wanted to help this young man find a more favorable, a more peaceful means of dealing with his dino angst, and his other frustrations in life. To find a more productive path than the perfect hook and jab he had developed.

I took my little slugger off to the side and knelt in front of him. His head hanging low, I sweetly shared what a nice young man I thought he was, and how happy I was to have him in my class. I asked what he liked to do most during our time together, and he brightened up and said, swinging outside. I let him know we would be doing that exact activity right after we cleaned up, and put the toys away. His head was lifted, and we were now eye to eye. Here's my chance to enlighten and engage.

"I have a favor to ask you," I said as he eagerly stared at me and while under the watchful eye of another teacher. One who thought the proper way to deal with all children was to swiftly escort them by the arm to sit in the corner… albeit since school rules frowned on hitting our tender tykes.

"The next time someone has something you want, or you feel angry, I would like you to count to 10, and come tell me." He agreed, and we cleaned up and went outside to play.

I felt pretty proud of myself having provided this little preschooler a useful tool to be used in life's moments of anger. Outside, the "mean" teacher and I talked. She was certain my way of doing things would not work. A proper spanking, and corner sit, was the order of the day for this young man. Counting to 10 does nothing for him, she debated. I held firm to my position and my teaching.

Within moments, my peace pilgrim prodigy comes running up to me with the enthusiasm of a Golden Retriever. "Mrs. Stephanie, Mrs. Stephanie, I did it." My heart swelled with pride as once again I knelt to hear the darling's "it" that he did. "I did it. I counted to 10, and then I hit him."

My teachings have gotten better and so have the results of those that follow them. Needless to say, I had more work to do with helping my students prepare for the pressures of preschool and life, but the principles are the same.

It is my intention to provide for you The Four Pillars of a Happy, Healthy Human. These Four Pillars are the exact same ones I offer to my clients throughout the United States and Europe, with men and women, with CEOs, doctors, lawyers, secretaries, truck drivers, and with just other hard-working folks, teenagers, children, teachers, and of course, friends and loved ones.

These Four Pillars are useful, practical, and easily implemented. If you made it through preschool, or kindergarten (even if you got held back), you can apply the Four Pillars for a Happy Healthy Human.

I will provide examples from my own life, my coaching practice, and specific scientific research that explains why the particular techniques I share works, and how to implement the Four Pillars into your daily life.

As I tell my clients and participants, "Knowledge is useful only when it is applied. Our doing is our applied knowing." It is not enough to read through the pages and set the book aside. This is a "doing" book. This is your opportunity to finally start living the life you want, feeling happy, healthy, and human!

What I discovered during my research were habits that we need to develop to alleviate the conditions that our bodies experience daily. These habits are not hard, or costly, and don't take much time. I am not going to tell you that you can't do certain things, or you have to overhaul your entire lifestyle. You don't. You don't have to be perfect either, because my friend, none of us are. Even if your mother insists that you are.

However, the benefits of applying just an "ounce" of the recommended Four Pillars concepts are worth a "pound" of benefits. Being a Happy, Healthy Human is well within reach and available to you right now. Wherever you are. Whatever the current state you find yourself in.

DEFINING HAPPY, HEALTHY, AND HUMAN

"Anything you may hold firmly in your imagination can be yours."
- William James

Happiness is a state of mind of pleasure, flourishing, or contentment. Happiness is experienced when we feel safe, satisfied, or successful. Happiness is often expressed with a smile as a way of being. Happy people have good energy, feel good.

A bit more on happiness. I disagree that our sole goal in life should be to "be happy." Feeling good, yes. However, feeling good, or feeling better, doesn't always equate to feeling happy. I give you and all my clients full permission to express emotions. Sometimes it feels better to be mad or angry rather than being stuck in despair or resentment.

Happiness is a way of being along the journey, not the destination per se. There is a lot of road between desire, knowing what you want or where you want to go, and satisfaction, which is often equated with happiness. I invite you to loosen your grip on "having to be happy," to sit back and enjoy the ride, knowing if you are in a valley (unhappy) and that you will soon be climbing out. Do not expect happiness every minute of every day. Happiness and health will always be in a constant state of flux.

Health is not just the absence of disease but complete mental, physical, and emotional well-being. Well-being is the term I like to use most as it encompasses our whole self. If you find yourself in a current state of mal-being, that's okay; it is just a temporary assessment. There is recovery from simple illness or injury as well as recovery from more serious or debilitating states of ill health. Again, it is important to assess what you want and where you are now. Your health, like your happiness, is subject to change!

Being human is beyond being a Homo sapiens or Hominidae (the great apes, or hominids). Being human is more in line with the "wise man," as coined by the naturalist Carl Linnaeus. Being human is being compassionate, sympathetic, generous, and forgiving.

Unlike other mammals, animals, or life forms that we know of, human beings are unique. We are unique from all other mammals in our ability to imagine and reflect and create from these thoughts. Being a happy, healthy human is someone who feels good, has internal controls for reflection and imagination, and a willingness to make a choice. A happy, healthy human is satisfied with what is now, but eager for more.

In "The History and Evolution of Life Coaching", Williams and Davis demonstrated one's effectiveness and success at work, stemmed not from knowing how to do the job better, but from their interpersonal relationships... one's beliefs of themselves, and their lifestyle.

Research concludes that POSSIBILITY thinking, coupled with accountability, challenged participants to do, and be, their very best. This results in career/business success as well as success in health, relationships, and a feeling of contentment and personal power. As a coach, I always look at a client's entire life... we see the whole person... not bits and pieces. What this means, for example, is looking at lack of sleep, uncovering how diet, exercise, environment, and the person's unique chronology plays a role... it's not as simple as offering a prescription "to get more sleep" or take a pill. This is why I love what I do.

I love the detective aspects of the work, the uniqueness of each person and situation. Sometimes a simple modification in a diet does the trick... like limiting caffeine after a certain hour or simply going to bed later... not earlier!

There truly is "no one size fits all." There's fun and excitement in the search... how boring would it be to be so alike that we shared the same answers to every question on our paths. Of course, there are very simple blanket behaviors that benefit everyone like clean water, real food, healthy air to breath... but these of course are basic. Health is not the mere absence of disease but a childlike exuberance for a life full of meaning, connection, and self-expression.

I have taken Maslow's basic level of human potential and turned it into The Four Pillars of Health. They are: Thinking, Breathing, Nourishment, and Rest. Now, let me introduce you to the four pillars of being a Happy, Healthy Human.

INTRODUCTION TO THE FOUR PILLARS OF WELL-BEING

The techniques I provide are free, easy, and don't take much time. Thinking, Breathing, Nourishing, and Rest are all you need to put in place to be a Happy, Healthy Human. I start at the top! With our head. Your thinking habits, mindset, world view, whatever you want to call it, either contribute to your overall well-being or destroy it.

Your breathing is next in line as we move down the body, and much of what we can't immediately control with our thinking, our breathing can usher in immediate relief. I will share several breathing techniques with you, including my favorite, that many of my clients report as being highly beneficial. Often we discount the most helpful opportunities we have because they don't cost much. If you insist on paying for your health, I will be happy to accept your money. You can find out how to reach me at the end of the book.

As we head into the third pillar, Nourish, don't panic. I am not going to say you have to eat a certain diet, or never indulge in your favorite foods or drinks. I share an important rule when it comes to a healthy eating plan. In addition, NOURISH is not just about food. We need tools to nourish relationships, dreams, and our *chosen* lifestyle.

The fourth pillar, Rest, is highly important, and the most overlooked and dismissed by the health and wellness community. However, studies are showing rest is more important to our overall well-being than exercise. Most of my clients report being too exhausted to follow exercise recommendations. I will cover sleep, as well as daily habits that will yield a peaceful slumber, so you have the needed brain function and energy to live happy and healthy.

There are unlimited positive practices we can participate in to contribute to being a happy, healthy human. I actually have a quick top 100 Positive Practices guide if you are interested. Go to BolsterUp.com for more information. Let's get a good understanding of the Four Pillars of a Happy Healthy Human.

The acronym I use with my Pillars is T-B-N-R2. The R is RR, and it's a repeat. We have T for thinking, B for breathing, N for nourishment, R for rest and then repeat. Those four pillars of positive practices will do more for you than any other diet or exercise program, or any other life skill. Without those four, without enough positive practices, without the four pillars in your life, you're prone to sickness and unhappiness. There is so much to be thankful for on this playground we call life, and you were meant to enjoy it. You were meant to feel good, to express yourself, and to explore. I want you to love life, love being a happy, healthy human.

The Four Pillars of Natural Healing: Thinking, Breathing, Nourishing, and Rest are your building blocks to a firm foundation of health and happiness.

CHAPTER 2

STRESS, THE COMMON DENOMINATOR

> *"The greatest weapon against stress is our ability to choose one thought over another."*
> **- William James**

Where did my concept of the Four Pillars originate? Most of my work for the last twenty years or so has been on stress, and more importantly, stress management for disease control and general unhappiness. I happened upon most of what has become the Four Pillars for a Happy, Healthy Human reviving my own mind and body from a devastating autoimmune disorder made worse by unhappy thinking habits. Most of us just refer to our unhappiness and illness as stress.

Stress is a major factor in our lives and can rob us of all we desire and want. Stress keeps us trapped, unhappy, and confused.

The United Nations has declared stress a worldwide epidemic, and most doctors and researchers have concluded that stress is responsible for over 80 to 90% of all illnesses and diseases.

Most of us are suffering each and every day because we don't understand the mechanisms of stress; mental, emotional, and physical. More importantly, most of us don't know about or use tools and techniques that provide relief, health, and happiness.

Our lives are stressful to our bodies. They really were not meant to be under this constant fight or flight status. The hormones that kick in were supposed to help us make quick decisions and then return to a normal baseline.

That is not what is happening in the majority of our lives. We get up, we are rushed through our morning, we get to work after sitting in traffic, our boss tells us that the report we're about to turn in has to be rewritten... all by noon. By the time we get home, we have to rush through dinner.

The underlying mechanism to our "stressed out" lives is NOT what you think it is. It is NOT all the outward ongoings of life. It is not your work or your relationship dynamics, it is not the traffic, learning new skills and knowledge in school, it is not the daily "grind" of life. If it is NOT all the outward life situations, then what is all the stress we experience and are trying to "manage" daily? I know this may sting a little, so brace yourself. It is your *thinking* and internal beliefs, self-talk, and how you manage your emotions that dictate whether a situation in life is stressful or not. Don't worry... you will have the necessary tools to manage your internal structure, so your life is actually more satisfying, fun, and pleasurable!

TYPICAL EXPERIENCES OF STRESS

Like me, you're trying to work, get your kids where they need to be, maybe trying to provide a healthy meal, keep your boss off your back, spend some quality time with a significant other, and oh yeah, remember trash day, which bills are due, and maybe have some leftover energy to actually exercise like you keep saying. Busy busy busy. Our body receives that busy busy busy as stress stress stress, and it doesn't have a chance, a long enough chance, to cool off. We go to bed hoping to be one of the lucky ones to capture a full night of sleep so we can actually feel better tomorrow.

This type of lifestyle will rob you of your health, happiness, and humanity. I have worked with organizations and individuals for the last 25 years on stress, health and daily outcomes. *Dying For A Paycheck: How Modern Management Harms Employee Health And Company Performance And What We Can Do About It* (HarperCollins, March 2018) author, Jeffrey Pfeffer highlights the negative phenomenon of stress related to work. I wrote my thesis on workplace stress, the substantial cost to lives, employers, communities, and the world. However, there is hope and lots of it, plenty to go around and share, and plenty of hope to last and keep you going tomorrow and the day after that. I am thrilled to be here with you and provide useful tools and techniques to help you be a happier, healthier human!

Most of us can't rewrite our whole day, we can't dictate what the weather's going to do or when we are going to receive a bad phone call or if the kids are going to miss the bus, getting stuck in heavy traffic…or if your boss, husband, or coworker is having a bad day.

All these events are happening that we have to deal with throughout our life. But there are things that we can put in place. There are positive practices that we can implement to help reduce the effects of stress on our bodies. It's so important that we do these and do them consistently. Develop these little habits of healthfulness to encourage your body to return to that calm-centered state that it so wants to get to throughout your day.

After my diagnosis with an autoimmune disorder (which I no longer have), I had my third baby and moved to another state that same weekend. Talk about stress! I'll tell you about that some other time. Let's just say I'm not immune to stress; I don't have a stress-free life.

What I do have are tools and techniques that allow my body to return to that calm state needed for healing, happiness and my overall human enjoyment of life. And again, that's what I'm going to share with you throughout this book.

So, no matter where you find yourself in life right now. If you're rushing through your hectic day, my heart feels for you. I definitely feel that. I understand that. If you find yourself in a diseased state or with an illness, I can definitely help you deal with that as well.

It is no fun to go through this wonderful life not feeling good. We're meant to have fun and to enjoy our lives and for life to be satisfying.

Life is not supposed to be a grind and a drain and just getting through the next day to the next moment. It's supposed to feel good! Yes, we're going to have moments that feel sad or uneasy. But for the majority of your day in your life, it should be fun!

You should be feeling good, you should have a decent level of happiness with your day-to-day living. That's why I'm so passionate about implementing The Four Pillars throughout your day. To ensure that your day is full of satisfaction and all of the wonderful things that life has for us.

LESS STRESS FOR MORE LIVING

"Be not afraid of life. Believe that life is worth living, and your belief will help create the fact."
- **William James**

In the English language, stress is defined as any type of change that causes physical, emotional or psychological strain. When an event happens that causes you to expend more energy, you experience stress. A certain level of stress is good for you.

This is called eustress or productive tension. At this stage, hormones are released into the body to give you an energy boost. These hormones enable you to "fight" or "flight." After you have expended the energy, you need to move below your normal stress level so that your nervous system can return to normal, and the "energy" hormones can dissipate and not be stored in the body. Your body is then able to return to a settled energy level and be ready for the next stressor in life. This is part of a healthy rhythm of well-being. Being able to move in and out of higher and lower energy life experiences with ease.

Here is what U.S. National Library of Medicine has to say about stress and hormones: "Psychological distress has been reported in up to 65% of younger patients. Severe stress may be a risk factor for diabetes. Mental stress leads to chronic activation of the neuroendocrine systems. Cortisol favors central fat deposition, a decrease in the adipostatic signal leptin, and an increase in the orexigenic signal ghrelin, inducing increased appetite and food intake. This phenomenon contributes to the current epidemic of obesity. In today's competitive modern world, one encounters stress in various aspects of life. As an adaptive response to stress, there is a change in the serum level of various hormones, including CRH, cortisol, catecholamines, and thyroid hormone. These changes may be required for the fight or flight response of the individual to stress. However, long-term exposure to stress may lead to many deleterious consequences leading to various endocrine disorders. Also, stress leads to change in the clinical course or status of many endocrine conditions."[2]

In other words, stress is bad for us, contributes to disease, unhealthy weight, and hormone malfunction. In response to stress, the level of various hormones changes. Reactions to stress are associated with enhanced secretion of a number of hormones, including glucocorticoids, catecholamines, growth hormone, and prolactin, the effect of which is to increase mobilization of energy sources and adapt the individual to its new circumstance.

The event creating the stress will be called a stressor and this can be from an inside or outside source. The behavior exhibited when stress occurs is defined as a stress reaction.

One important thing to note is that the body cannot tell the difference between an actual stressor and an imagined one. Let me repeat this... the body cannot tell the difference between an actual stressor and an imagined one.

This is why you might feel fatigued after watching a scary or intense movie or thinking about past traumas. It is very real to your body! This is why our thinking is vital to happiness and health. We can think about unpleasant ideas, and our body will respond with a stress response.

---

[2] (Jan-Mar & 18–22.)

What you may not understand are the serious implications that stress can have on our overall health. With the escalating cost of health care, it would serve us well to focus our attention on understanding stress and becoming better educated regarding our ability to manage it.

And then comes, of course, the need to follow through by implementing what we have learned. The tools and techniques I am giving you now are mighty in their magic to keep stress at bay and decrease the effects of stress on your physical body.

Often stress is related to all the things we are thinking about that aren't going right. Our stress is related to all the demands we have in our lives and the lack of resources to meet those demands.

TYPES OF STRESS

"It's not stress that kills us; it is our reaction to it."
- Hans Selye

Let's further explore two of the most common types of stress as you experience them in your daily life.

Acute stress is a reaction to an immediate, unexpected stressor, like:

- Seeing a child run into a busy street
- Hearing a loud noise

- A phone call telling you of an emergency situation

- Being unexpectedly called on to speak

- A very verbal, highly irritated customer

- Being pulled out of the airport security line for extensive screening

- Learning that your credit card was declined

During acute stress, an unexpected event occurs, you have the appropriate hormonal response, and you respond at a higher energy level. Then when the event is over, you seek out the first chance to relax. The body can deal with acute stress in small doses. But prolonged bouts of acute stress are very taxing to the body.

Chronic Stress is prolonged stress. There seems to be no light at the end of the tunnel. You don't feel any hope for the future and feel that you have no power over the situation. Some situations that produce chronic stress are:

- Being homeless

- No perceived power in a relationship or job

- Dysfunctional or abusive family

- Trapped in a despised job or career

For most people, though, chronic stress is more often a product of:

- Too much to do, too many commitments with no end in sight

- Working longer hours on the job with little or no reward

- Too little sleep for days and weeks at a time

- Disorganization in our living and work environments

- Financial problems that are worsening by the month

- Fear of losing a job

- Prolonged illness (yours or a family member)

While we cannot control all the stressors in our life, we can control how we respond to them. There are numerous techniques you can practice to protect your well-being despite the challenges that come your way. Remember, ultimately, you choose how you will respond to the circumstances in your life.

Many events in life are unpleasant, but the majority of our uneasiness stems from our lack of commitment to what we want in life. I call the goals or aspirations of what we really want our REAL SELF. Most of us are at a loss for what we want. I will address this later in the book in more depth. The comprehensive video course is another great resource and the next step after reading the book.

INFLAMMATION AND STRESS

A little background on unhappiness and health. It is now established that disease, particularly chronic or autoimmune disorders are a byproduct of inflammation. Inflammation is a result of many factors, including your thinking, breathing, eating, environment, and resting habits. Inflammation also settles into the most vulnerable or weakest areas in your body.

The big issue with inflammation, long-term or chronic, is it destroys our cells. THIS IS HUGE!!!

in ·flam ·ma ·tion/ ˌinflə'māSH(ə)n/

Noun: a localized physical condition in which part of the body becomes reddened, swollen, hot, and often painful, especially as a reaction to injury or infection.

Short-term inflammation is a wonderful tool used by your body when it is trying to rid itself of an offending agent.

> *"Inflammation is the body's attempt at self-protection; the aim being to remove harmful stimuli, including damaged cells, irritants, or pathogens — and begin the healing process."*
> - **Christian Nordqvist**

As a body becomes overwhelmed with too many offending agents for prolonged periods, it will suffer. Let's pause a minute and clarify some terms. I'll start with the word "overwhelmed."

How often do we say we are overwhelmed or hear others with this battle cry? Being or feeling overwhelmed comes from not having the resources to meet demands. This resource can be time, money, physical strength, or mental capacity.

When our bodies reach a tipping point, the inflammation settles and destroys cells, often resulting in disease. I equate inflammation to stress and our body's inability to handle a "toxic load." As long as our bodies can handle the load then we can maintain health.

However, as soon as our system becomes overrun with a toxic load, we will become ill. The body is unable to discard the "inflammation, stress" in efficient ways and the scales tip to the side of disease.

I will use toxins and offending agents interchangeably throughout this book. Although a toxin can indicate a more dangerous offending agent, for our purposes, they will mean the same thing. I do this because an offending agent is a toxin for one person but perhaps not toxic to another. For example, peanuts. Many thrive on this legume, whereas others are so "offended" they may not survive unless intervention is taken.

Offending agents can also be our thoughts and feelings, which can be wildly different from one person to the next. There are 12 "Destructive Dozen" thoughts that plague the majority of us. (See Appendix). The online course covers how to appropriately acknowledge and deal with the Destructive Dozen. Our minds and body are always collaborating, looking for how to behave, act and feel. This is also the reason the tools and techniques I use in this book can be seen as holistic and allopathic. I take a holistic mind, body, and scientific approach to well-being.

So, what exactly creates a toxic load or too much for your body or mind to handle? This is where life gets interesting because it is different for each of us. Some things are going to present too much for anybody to handle, and we are going to get sick, or die. For example, cyanide will kill any healthy adult... an extreme example of a toxic load. Your body is not able to rid itself fast enough of the offending agent.

But not all potentially offending agents actually kill the host. In fact, although very rare, there have even been a few bodies that were able to survive cyanide poisoning. I find it very interesting that some folks are able to survive the potential for a deadly toxic agent while many or most succumb.

For instance, another example of a foreign agent that creates a toxic load is the bacteria known as Yersinia pestis.

Many died, but others were able to outpace its deadly effects. Why do some succumb to such awful epidemics and others thrive?

Our best information to date, according to Black Death expert Sharon DeWitte, is the bacteria became a deadly toxic load to those already with compromised systems. In other words, it was the tipping point for some and just a nuisance for others if there was any suffering at all. For systems already treading water, another "offending agent" was just too much and overwhelmed or drowned the system.

The same is true today. The COVID 19 pandemic is the first that many in 2021 have ever experienced. Again, the first to fall to the attack were the same in other pandemics as well.

Although we are all subject to toxic overloading, the other truth is we have amazing bodies! Our bodies do a great job keeping us alive and ridding our system of offending agents without us ever being aware or knowing what the latest "attack" was. However, like the already weakened systems and bodies that fall from the Plague, Coronavirus or other widely offending agents, our bodies can only take so much.

There is a tremendous amount of hope in what we can do to strengthen our immune system and decrease inflammation. This is the heart of the Four Pillars to well-being. We all have tremendous control over our thinking, breathing, nourishment, and rest which results in each of us being stronger, and our bodies more easily "dumping" the waste from offending agents.

Let's dive a little deeper into the stress response.

STRESS AND TENSION

Now that we have covered some of what stress is and what stress does, I want to introduce you to another concept. The idea of stress creates tension, and tension seeks relief. Most of us have "snapped" at someone at some point in our lives. Like a rubber band pulled on, it seeks release and will "snap" back to a state of less tension, or less stress, or what I call ease. We ease the tension by snapping. The "snap" can be a sharp tone and hurtful words, a few too many glasses of wine, or frequent visits to the pantry to ease the tension with crunchy chips.

The issue is we feel better initially by the "snap," or a release, but in the long run, we know we reacted out of a build-up of tension and not from a place of ease and calm. This becomes the difference between reacting versus responding. It is simply a structure. The good news is structure, or how we release, "real ease" into a response is malleable.

We want to respond to life's events. Responding requires a thoughtful, conscious choice of action. However, to get to a state of responding and not merely reacting involves 4 key elements or pillars of well-being. I reveal in the pages ahead the process, science, real-life examples, and practices to implement to help live that life you want now…

CHAPTER 3

PILLAR I: THINKING

> *"A positive attitude causes a chain reaction of positive thoughts, events and outcomes. It is a catalyst and it sparks extraordinary results."*
> - **Wade Boggs**

You will learn:

- Design your life for what works for you
- Compassion is the key… it broadens your perspective
- leading to better decision making

The first pillar I'm going to share with you is your thinking. Your head sits on top of your shoulders for a reason. There are several tools, techniques, and practices that can be used to shift our thinking. Meditation and mindfulness are all the craze right now, for a good reason. They work. However, other shifts in our thinking that lead toward happier, healthier living include communication in our physical form and environment.

Just by adjusting our body posture or moving to a different environment, like going outside or to a different room, can support a shift in our thinking.

How we react to stress is contingent on our world view, outlook on life, or what we think. How we react, or hopefully respond, is always our choice. When we start to separate others' behaviors, actions and communication from our own, we take control of our internal world and free ourselves to behave in ways that feel good. Let's explore a very worthwhile tool for adjusting your thinking structure.

WHAT MINDFULNESS IS AND HOW TO USE IT

The new buzzword for this is your mindset, or *your way of thinking*. Our thinking is even more important than exercise to our health! What and how we think is the cornerstone to everything good or bad in our life. We must give more attention to how we think.

With my four pillars of well-being our thinking naturally comes first, as our thoughts create our reality. For example, if food is not readily available, I must think of a way to acquire it. Perhaps I have the means to purchase some food (I must also mentally prepare myself for "what" I will purchase). I must figure out how I will find, pick, capture, or kill and prepare some food, or how to get out of my current situation to have more food available to me. Our thinking comes first and cannot be dismissed or overlooked. Before going to a grocery store, one must think about what food is best, safe, and in line with what is needed. This is true for all our unwanted situations be they related to health, relationship or finance. A successful hunter will think like his prey, outsmart the moves, and successfully obtain a meal. The same type of thinking is needed for foraging as well, thinking about where edible sources of nutrients can be found and acquired. As a coach, it is this first pillar that must be addressed before proceeding to anything else. Our thoughts are our basis for all our behavior, choices, and ultimately, our lifestyle...good or bad. I'd like to take a moment and address some common issues with our thinking, especially when the thoughts are creating unwanted or negative behaviors and life circumstances. Without a doubt, cultural influence, as well as our upbringing, contribute a great deal to our pattern of thinking.

How to change your thinking. I could write a whole book, and many have: *Psycho-Cybernetics* by Maxwell Maltz; *Mindset: The New Psychology of Success* by Carol Dweck; *The Astonishing Power of Emotions: Let Your Feelings Be Your Guide* by Esther and Jerry Hicks.

The overwhelming outcome of the research, studies, and testing concludes that our thinking can be altered, changed, and new more helpful and successful patterns can be created. The effect is a new structure, therefore new experience. A new wanted, thoughtful, and considerate experience that creates health, happiness and joy.

Do we see the glass half full or half empty? Did that guy deliberately cut you off in traffic, or was he just not paying attention? Did your husband want to hurt your feelings by forgetting your birthday, or was he just overwhelmed with all that he has going on?

Our thinking and thoughts have a great deal to do with the stress in our lives, or at least how we deal with it. There are many worthwhile reasons to explore stress management techniques that are beneficial for you.

A lot of our thinking habits are not so great for our happiness or health, although they are human. Most of what I teach as a speaker and coach about our thinking is really about being aware of how you are feeling!

Most of your life is created by your thoughts. Your thinking and outlook on life directly influence the choices you make, the relationships you have or don't have. And importantly, your thoughts contribute greatly to illness and diseases. Your thoughts can also reverse sickness and pain, creating healing and happiness.

The most successful and healthiest people have a particular thinking pattern. When they're faced with obstacles or things that don't go their way, they have an automatic focus on looking for solutions.

They don't spend a lot of time thinking about the negative aspects of the problem or situation. They certainly don't spend a lot of time pointing fingers and blaming people. Now, I don't want you to get hung up on that. This is all a part of being a human being. If you're not aware of your thought patterns, then how are you going to shift them, or neutralize them, or create healthier new ones?

I'm going to show you some very simple techniques and procedures that you can start implementing today that will help you shift your focus from a negative to a positive one. If you're not particularly aware of the negative things that are running around in your head on a daily basis, the BolsterUP online course provides more detailed instructions and awareness lessons.

It is necessary to be gentle with yourself right now. If you are aware or *think* you have negative thinking habits, that's okay. No need to beat yourself up about it. Instead, pat yourself on the back and give yourself some credit that you are here now. Right now, just by reading this book, you are opening up your thinking and will benefit from the exposure, even if you choose not to follow through on all the recommendations.

Unhealthy thinking habits make you feel trapped and constricted. Healthy thinking habits make you feel free, happy, at ease. Good thinking understands that there's a solution to your problems or ways around obstacles that you are facing.

So, if you feel trapped and constricted, then we know that there's a need to shift your thinking. You always have a choice about what you're thinking. If you don't like some of the thoughts running through your head, pick some new ones! I know that sounds simple, and it takes some practice to start implementing, but you can do it!

You always have a choice about what you're thinking. No more stinkin' thinkin'! We are going to throw stinkin' thinkin' out. It is your brain, and you have the right to control it. Health and happiness are yours for the taking. They're yours for the thinking!

Long ago, when I was introduced to this information, I thought that was impossible, and I couldn't quite wrap my mind around it. When I started practicing some of these techniques that I'm going to share with you, eventually, my body started to respond to my thinking. So, let's get into the first tool to shift your thinking from negative to positive.

You have this beautiful brain of yours to help you to heal and to live in happiness, have success and fulfillment. You can use your thinking to either help you or to hurt you.

YOUR THINKING IS YOUR CHOICE

> *"The art of being wise is the art of knowing*
> *what to overlook."*
> - **William James**

One of the difficulties I had in changing my thinking habits to help my healing was noticing my thoughts. Perhaps you don't notice your unhealthy thinking habits. I have a few tools for you that I will cover in this chapter.

Which statement most likely describes your reaction in a typical day:

"It's hopeless; there is no way it can be done."

Or...

"There is a solution to every problem, and I am confident we can figure this out."

How about these:

"I'm poor and never have enough money."

Or...

"I feel wealthy, and I have a lot of wonderful things."

"I'm sick and tired of being the only one who does anything around here."

Or...

"I am surrounded by helpful, kind people."

These attitude statements have a tremendous effect on your life. Happy, healthy people have a good attitude and mindset. They consistently look for solutions to problems instead of someone or something to blame. Having a positive attitude is essential for happiness and health. The great news is that your attitude is a habit and can be improved upon. Mine sure did.

Carol Dweck, Ph.D. who studies the psychology of success, boils mindset down to two camps: fixed or growth. I'll refer to a positive mindset as a growth mindset.

The first step in establishing a positive mindset or attitude is becoming aware of your current go-to methods. What happens when someone spills the milk, or cuts you off in traffic, or picks you up late? How do you feel when faced with obstacles such as your car not starting, or finding out you just lost your primary income, or your spouse doesn't want the same things you do?

Having a positive attitude doesn't mean you don't honor your feelings. Quite the opposite. In fact, it is very important to acknowledge all your emotions and give voice to even the ones we often term as negative.

All emotions are necessary and are just messengers. We experience positive emotions like love, hope, confidence, gratefulness, satisfaction when our needs are being met. And negative emotions like fear, frustration, anger, loneliness, anxiety, guilt, or withdrawal when our needs are not being met.

So a great tool to start with is assessing needs being met, needs not being met. That's it. This assessment alone can provide some space for a response verses a reaction.

I do prefer the term growth mindset to positive mindset for a few reasons. One is the stigma of having a positive mindset often equates to images of a cheerleader type without acknowledging anything other than a happy face, and upbeat, high spirited demeanor. Secondly, there is no hope for one that finds they do not "have a positive mindset." A growth mindset does the opposite. It can take whatever is experienced, failure, frustration, etc. and then asks the following questions: Is this experience based on facts? Have I approached the issue from more than one angle? What resources are available to assist me? A growth mindset then produces self-talk that is helpful, not harmful, like the following:

"I can learn from this."

"Life is full of challenges that can be fun."

"I can apply myself more to the task."

"What are the benefits to what I am experiencing?"

Having a growth mindset starts with recognizing your thoughts and feelings. The positive aspects come into play with what you do with those thoughts and feelings. Remember, successful, happy people with a growth mindset focus on what they want, and look for solutions… not blame.

One day, I was over at a business partner's home. My son was about one and a half, and he was with me. My partner and I had a lot of business to discuss and plans to go over, and we were sitting at her kitchen table. We lived in Arizona, and many people had water delivery services because the water was extremely harsh, and you needed to filter it before using it for drinking or cooking.

Well, she had this very large jug that sat on a stand, and you flipped a valve down for the water to flow out. While we were focused on our conversation, my son, who was just a few feet away and within eyesight, was flipping the valve up and down. Before my partner and I realized the kitchen floor was flooded.

I was horrified. I felt so embarrassed and a bit worried because I knew these large water jugs cost a lot of money, and it was all over her floor. I didn't feel the need to punish my son, he was just playing and being curious, but I felt awful. My partner and friend didn't miss a beat. She smiled and shrugged. "Well, my floors needed to be cleaned anyway." She got some towels, and we all cleaned up the water. Her reaction had a big impact on me. I have known all too well many who would have been very upset and even angry, yelled at the child, and still have had to clean up the water.

I noticed three things about her response versus my reaction.

- It alleviated my initial anxiety and ill feelings.

- We all smiled and had a good time.

- The water got cleaned up.

This woman was a very successful business owner and a happy, healthy, beautiful person. She wasn't without troubles, struggles, or obstacles. But she met life with a problem-solving attitude and didn't look for blame. She could have easily been very upset with my son and me for not being more aware of what he was doing.

We can all adopt this way of thinking and being. The water wasn't going back in the jug. It wasn't even an option. She found a way to maintain a good mood while solving the problem.

I wouldn't classify myself as an angry person... but I can go from 0-60 in one second flat. I can get really mad really fast, but unlike others, I don't hold a grudge. I am like a little firecracker. Once it pops, it's done.

Over the years, I have had to own this and alter my mindset and reaction.

As a child, I learned to be very reactive. It worked most of the time and pushed me to get things done. I used to clean if I got very angry about something. Have you ever seen how fast an angry woman can clean a kitchen? It worked for me, or I thought it did.

I would also project way into the future what could happen if something didn't go as I wanted it to. I was very good at this in high school. I convinced myself that if I got a B or C, I would never get into college, I would never get married. If I didn't get all As, I would end up homeless.

Stop for a minute and think about the last time you got angry over something. Anything big or small. What was your reaction? Just notice what you said or thought and the actions you took. Most of the time, the result is the same...the water must be cleaned up. BUT, your attitude about it makes all the difference to health, wealth, and happiness.

My harmful thinking patterns included constantly telling myself that I wasn't lovable, hating my body, and always trying to be thinner. The biggest mindset was that I was not worthy of health, happiness, or helping.

The inability to ask for and receive help is a tremendous hindrance to growth. We are social creatures and feel the most alive, healthy, and honored when we serve others and can openly and enthusiastically receive as well. Like a golden retriever open to receive love and affection... from anyone!

How many people do you know who shy away from compliments or assistance? Perhaps you have difficulty asking for help. This need to do it all myself and do it perfectly nearly cost me my life. It cost me my health for sure, was destroying my relationships, and kept me from cultivating the friendships I wanted.

It's time to end stinkin' thinkin' and create a magnificent mood! The absolute fabulous news comes from much research in neuroplasticity. We can create new connections between neurons. This means we can change our outlook or mindset and mood with experience and with practice.

First is the noticing or mindfulness.

REAL LIFE STORY

My oldest daughter shared with me that she introduced The Nicest Things (found in the practical applications section in this chapter), a favorite "family ritual," at camp. Even the camp counselors and leaders got involved, and they continued to ask and answer the three questions each time they had a meal... yes, three questions, three times a day! WOW. I was so proud of my daughter for extending this powerful mindful tool to her peers and instructors.

As a communication tool to shift our thinking from negative to positive, this is fast and effective. Many of my clients use The Nicest Things with their spouses. One client, a busy oncologist, was struggling with communication with her spouse. They had the usual busy schedules of two professionals trying to raise children and still trying to understand and listen. To her surprise, not only did she and her husband start sharing more, they learned more about each other and started celebrating what was going well. As a matter of fact, she reported being pleasantly surprised when going to bed and not sharing The

Nicest Things, her husband told her he missed the interaction. This very small but deliberate exchange has greatly improved the way they think about the other, and each has agreed to continue the practice daily. I want you to ask yourself these three questions every day! Make it a family practice at the dinner table. That is what I do. When my children have friends over for dinner, they eagerly look forward to sharing their answers. Here they are. What is the nicest thing you did for someone today? What is the nicest thing someone did for you? What is the nicest thing you did for yourself?

Many of my clients come to me wanting to make a change to live happier, healthier, and more meaningful lives. Language, words is another tool for a happy, healthy human experience. One of my clients came to me wanting to "lose" weight. The first thing I do with any of my weight "loss" clients is to help them switch from the negative language of what they don't want to a more positive language of what they do. I ask my clients if they have ever lost anything, a phone, keys, track of a child. Of course, we all have. I ask them to think about how they feel and what they do when they lose something. The answers are all the same, with varying degrees of discomfort from panicked to annoyed, but the key is we stop, search, and do all we can to get it back. The word "lose" is associated with a negative feeling and unproductive behavior. I guide my clients to find a word that feels better but achieves the desired result. Many come up with the word "release." Think about these two words, lose and release. Lose feels heavier, defeated, low. Nobody likes to lose. How about release? A much lighter word, uplifting even, higher if you will. When we lose something, we expect or want it back. When we release, the opposite is true, we make a decision to let it go and don't go searching for it anymore. Word choice is crucial to a growth mindset. Try to state what you do want in your speech and in your self talk.

I LIKE THE PAIN

We teach our brains and bodies what we choose to participate in and how much pain or pleasure we will derive from the experience. Take flying, for example. Some sit in their seats in sheer terror, hands clutching the armrests or nails digging into the flesh of the well-meaning comforting companion. Others sit with ease, passively paging through a magazine and seriously considering a cat relaxation pod for their precious Oliver, the friendly feline.

We teach ourselves pleasure and pain and convince ourselves situations will result in one or the other. "I hate flying," you say. Well, your mind, your brain, makes sure you have that experience. Compare "I hate flying" to "I think flying is fun and an easy way to get to where I want to go." These are two different directives, and your mind will obey your command or comments. Be careful what you say to yourself and to others, for you are creating your reality with your thinking.

I often tell my clients to picture themselves as a small child they are instructing, a provider and protector over. What would you say to that small child? Would you tell the child she is fat, stupid, or incapable? Would you spend hours convincing the child flying is not safe, is a hardship or burden, and should hate it although it's necessary to get to where they want or need to go? Seems a bit absurd, harsh and untruthful doesn't it? How often do we do this to ourselves because we are not mindful?

DETAILED SCIENTIFIC EVIDENCE

Carol Dweck, Ph.D., Stanford University Psychologist and author of *Mindset*, studies the psychology of success. For the past thirty years, Dr. Dweck has pioneered a new way of learning, and current neuroscience research backs up her original theory about success equating to a growth mindset and failure to a fixed one. What is exciting about Dweck's research and the backing of current neuroscience research on brain plasticity is that we can all achieve a more growth mindset and, therefore, more success with practice.

In 1984, Susan Folkman suggested that stress results from an imbalance between demands and resources or one's perceived ability to cope.

Most stress management techniques are developed based on the idea that stress is not a direct response to the stressor BUT one's resources and ability to cope with the perceived stressor. Take a moment and let this sink in. Stress is NOT the same for everyone. It is our reaction to what we think about what is happening.

Several disciplines and practices can cultivate mindfulness, such as Yoga, Tai Chi, and Qigong, but most of the literature has focused on mindfulness that is developed through mindfulness meditation — those self-regulation practices that focus on training attention and awareness to bring mental processes under greater voluntary control and thereby foster general mental well-being and development and/or specific capacities such as calmness, clarity, and concentration (Walsh & Shapiro, 2006).

I was particularly drawn to research (Dweck, Carol. (2019) where adolescent students improved grades and increased enrollment in advanced courses with less than one hour of Dweck's online training. Using a social psychological model addressing the beliefs teens had about intelligence, not a fixed trait but an effort issue, displaces beliefs that they are not capable of achieving more, when actually all of us are with the right mindset. Dweck's work boils down to "I can't" vs. "I can't yet." This powerful three-letter word creates such a different world for those that choose to use it. It is filled with the promise of improvement, growth, and achievement. In my coaching, I am firm about the language my clients use and spend a lot of time working this out; the words said out loud as well as the self-talk they choose to use. My clients see dramatic improvements in their lives just by choosing certain words over others. You can too.

Another mindfulness pioneer and researcher, The Mother of Mindfulness, Ellen Langer, has provided a rich research approach to how we make decisions. The conclusion is we all just need to be deliberate with our thinking and get out of autopilot. Choice is king and controls the magic of the kingdom. When we think we are making deliberate choices, we feel in control, whether we are or not or whether the outcome changes or not. Langer's first book, *Mindfulness*, published in 1989, is well worth reading. I also found *Counter Clockwise* to be inspiring. Dr. Langer's work is among many that reveal our thinking habits can contribute very significantly to our aging, health, and happiness.

Harvard Neuroscientist, Susan Lazar, shocked me with her research. Three powerful discoveries have come from monitoring brain scans. One, we can grow our brain! Yes, we can actually grow gray matter, and not only slow down the aging or atrophy of normal living, but after just eight weeks of meditation, the brain scans revealed no difference between a twenty-five-year-old and fifty-year-old's brain. Now that is powerful! However, Dr. Lazar's research on meditation has my attention for more than brain growth or plasticity abilities, but for the reduction of the amygdala. The second powerful discovery is not brain growth but a specific brain area shrinkage. The amygdala is larger in those who report being more stressed, anxious, or depressed. Lazar's brain scans reveal a lasting shrinkage of the amygdala after meditation. Again, this discovery is exciting because a smaller amygdala seems to support an individual's reported levels of stress and anxiety. The third powerful discovery of Susan Lazar's meditation (as well as other studies) is the reported benefit is a sense of calm. Even though circumstances have not changed, the meditators' *reaction* and ability to respond more peacefully, creatively, and compassionately has! The gray matter growth, the smaller the amygdala, the better we can handle the stresses and upsets of life. I want a younger brain, happier state, and overall healthier way of being, so I will definitely continue to meditate.

Researchers show that mindfulness meditation promotes awareness and understanding of one's own thought process. Meditation also decreases the thinking of the same issues, referred to as rumination. Meditation also seems to make paying attention easier.

More specifically, research on mindfulness has identified these benefits: Daphne M. Davis, PhD, and Jeffrey A. Hayes, PhD wrote an article that explored at all the ways mindfulness is beneficial including reduced rumination, stress reduction, boosts to working memory, focus, less emotional activity, more cognitive flexibility, relationship satisfaction, and other benefits. In addition the article explores benefits of empathy, compassion, decrease stress and anxiety as better quality of life.

Reduced rumination or thinking about something over and over or deeply. More often rumination shows up as negative self-talk. "Why am I so stupid" or cycling through a painful emotional experience long after it has passed. "I can't believe my lover treated me so terribly, how could he do that to me".

Several studies have shown that mindfulness reduces these negative, unhelpful ruminations. Chambers et al. (2008) asked 20 novice meditators to participate in a 10-day intensive mindfulness meditation retreat. The findings from the study showed decreased depression, less rumination, increased attention, and better memory. After the retreat, the meditation group had significantly higher self-reported mindfulness and a decreased negative effect compared with a control group. They also experienced fewer depressive symptoms and less rumination. In addition, the meditators had significantly better working memory capacity and were better able to sustain attention during a performance task compared with the control group.

Stress reduction. Many studies show that practicing mindfulness reduces stress. Mindfulness meditation increases positivity and decreases anxiety and negative emotion.

Participants in an eight-week mindfulness-based stress reduction group had neural reactivity measured by fMRI after watching sad films (Farb et al., 2010).

The participants who were using mindfulness-based stress reduction had significantly less anxiety, depression, and somatic distress compared with the control group. In addition, the fMRI data indicated that the mindfulness group had less neural re-activity when they were exposed to the films than the control group, and they displayed distinctly different neural responses while watching the films than they did before their mindfulness training. Wow! That is huge!

Another study from Johns Hopkins University published in JAMA Internal Medicine shows mindful meditation can help ease psychological stresses like anxiety, depression, and pain.

Boosts to working memory. Research finds improvements to working memory appear to be another benefit of mindfulness.

One study looked at a military group who participated in an eight-week mindfulness training. The military members improved working memory capacity as well an increase in positive emotion and decrease in negative.

Focus. Research shows mindfulness meditation affects participants' ability to focus attention and suppress distracting information. Another study found meditators had significantly better performance on all measures of attention and had higher self-reported mindfulness (Moore and Malinowski, 2009).

Less emotional reactivity. Emotion regulation is a central component of mental health. Those that practice mindfulness are better able to decrease emotional reactivity (Ortner et al., 2007).

More cognitive flexibility. In addition to being less reactive, people who practice mindfulness develop the skill of self-observation, which neurologically disengages the automatic pathways created by prior learning and enables present-moment input to be integrated in a new way (Siegel, 2007a). In other words, it is easier to learn new habits.

Relationship satisfaction. Of course it seems obvious the more aware of your emotions, less reactive you are, and better able to focus relates to relationship satisfaction because one is better able to respond to stress coupled with being better at communicating emotions to a partner. Empirical evidence suggests that mindfulness protects against the emotionally stressful effects of relationship conflict (Barnes et al., 2007), is positively associated with the ability to express oneself in various social situations (Dekeyser et al., 2008), and predicts relationship satisfaction (Barnes et al., 2007; Wachs & Cordova, 2007).

Other benefits. Mindfulness also reduces fear, has numerous health benefits, including increased immune functioning, decreases thoughts unrelated to tasks at hand, as well the effort to do the tasks. All mindfulness improves the overall well being of the participant.

I could fill the pages of another book on the neuroscience of stress and what stress does to our thinking and ability to function, heal, and even make decisions. It boils down to we are all walking chemical factories, and the hormonal (chemical) balance produced by our thinking makes a tremendous difference in how well we function as human beings.

As mentioned before, positive communication is a powerful indicator of our health and happiness. Our communication style or use of words is powerful. In a neurological experiment, Maria Richter and other scientists monitored brain activity when subjects heard or thought of negative words. The study revealed what many of us already know...negative words make us feel anxious or stressed. What is vital is that it doesn't matter where the negativity comes from — others or our own thoughts — when heard, our body releases stress and anxiety hormones.

For a real visual on the use of words and the possible response I love the work of Dr. Masaru Emoto words power on water. The imagery is fascinating

Now that you have an understanding of how vital your thinking is to your health, happiness and quality human experience let's explore how to implement positive practices.

PRACTICAL PRACTICE TO APPLY NOW

If you are aware or *think* you have negative thinking habits, that's okay, we all do or did at some point. No need to beat yourself up about it. Instead, pat yourself on the back and give yourself some credit that you are here now. Right now, just by reading this book, you are opening up your thinking and will benefit from the exposure even if you choose not to follow through on all the recommendations.

MINDFULNESS:

There are many practices we can apply to shift our thinking to a more beneficial habit. Here are three helpful and powerful ways to do just that. Mindfulness, questioning, and curiosity will get you moving in the right direction very quickly!

Although I am going to share more formal techniques, the first tool is great for beginners and anyone wanting an immediate shift.

If you're not ready or inclined to monitor your overall speech and clean up all the negativity, one simple word can increase a growth mindset, communication, and hope. The word is "yet." Just inserting this simple three-letter word into your thinking and speaking can improve your happiness, health, and humanity. It tells the story to you and others that you can... because you certainly can!

Another useful, easy to implement practice is to focus your attention on something other than "problems."

Start with what is going well. What is currently working? This is great for your overall life, as well as business success. Just by looking around for what is already working shifts everything! Changes your perspective and allows you to then explore how to "get" or "do" more of that. It is a fabulous way to structure any strategy session too. And before you protest, there is *always* something working, or going well. If you need to start with simple basics do so, like your breathing, the toilet flushes, employees showing up for work, plenty of air to breathe. Just look for it.

Another quick process of change that will help you no matter what kind of day you are having or what illness you are faced with is changing the word "stress" to "fear." Anytime you would use the word stress, say fear. By making the shift from stress to fear you are closer to identifying a need that needs to be met. And then you can start to identify ways to meet that need.

For more formal practices in healthier thinking try these suggestions. Let's start with the key to all good thinking and behavior... mindfulness or noticing without judgment. First is the noticing or mindfulness part. Here is what I mean by mindfulness. All mindfulness is, is noticing the sensory details or even your thoughts. Second is to notice without judging them. The key is NOT TO JUDGE, JUST NOTICE. What this means is not apply opinions to what you are noticing. This can be tricky. It's helpful to apply sensory detail when you are noticing. For example, you can notice how something feels cold, soft, sticky, or hard. Not, this is cold, and I don't like it, or this is sticky and gross.

I have my clients focus on just one sensory detail, like sight, sound or touch or feeling. You can focus on just one or several. I prefer when I am being deliberate to focus on one sensory detail at a time and really pay attention to it, try to describe it even apply color to it if there is none.

If you have ever arrived somewhere and did not remember the trip, or if you can't remember who was at an event after it was over, you will benefit from practicing mindfulness. Mindfulness is a technique where you give full attention to your feelings, thoughts, environment, and other sensations.

> *"The good news is that mindfulness is a state and not a trait."*

Mindfulness focuses awareness without judgement, that's it. You can become aware of the sensation of holding this book, or the type on the page, or the sound of the air circulating from the vent. However, mindfulness is different from meditation.

MEDITATION

I view meditation as a more formal practice of mindfulness. It is a scientific method for organizing and training the mind. This is why those with depression, and focus issues benefit. Meditation also makes us kinder and more humane. Meditation is definitely a process for happy, healthy and human living. There are two broad styles of meditation. The first is what most of us think about when we hear "meditation" and is passive with the goal of clearing the mind. The second style is active meditation, or dynamic meditation as promoted by Mind Valley creator and owner, Vishen Lakhiani. As a busy woman, and business owner I am starting to utilize more dynamic meditative practices in my life as do other highly successful - or want to be highly successful - entrepreneurs.

Meditation is a deliberate act of being still, at some point with your eyes closed, and focusing on letting go of thoughts. It is necessary to be gentle with yourself when beginning any form of meditation practice.

You literally remain "in the moment" and heighten your *consciousness* of everything around you. This exercise takes very little time, but the benefits are tremendous. Although the goal for many meditators is enlightenment, my goal for you is improved overall life satisfaction, and health.

To practice meditation, you must be willing to not let other things distract you. If your cell phone rings, you simply acknowledge to yourself that your phone is ringing, but don't let your mind wonder who is calling. Simply notice without judgement and return your attention to your breathing or focus.

For greater insight an incredibly helpful tool for meditating is John Yate's book, *The Mind Illuminated*. Yates is a neuroscientist and master meditator, not only does he offer a helpful 10 stage model for meditating but great parables to teach your consciousness how to control the meditation practice. And if you want to get to the highest level of enlightenment Yates' book is a great guide to do so.

MINDFULNESS EXERCISES

There are many ways to meditate. You have more Zen, just sit style, and others that offer vibrant visualizations. None are wrong. But in an effort to begin somewhere you can start with the following.

MEDITATIVE AWARENESS

Time: 1 minute

During this exercise, look around. Notice the variations of color in the room. Listen intently for any sounds. Notice the feel of the air on your body. Be still, as if you are becoming a part of your surroundings.

Be aware of your breathing. Hear the clock tick or the birds chirp. Notice how light reflects, distorts, or illuminates. See what you haven't seen before. Pick up an object like a pen or pencil and focus on all the details, color, weight, texture, try to notice as many sensory details as possible. Appreciate your surroundings and feel peace.

Self-talk is exactly what the term implies. It is the thousands of things we say to ourselves each day. Self-talk is about judgement. Judging ourselves and judging others.

Make a commitment to pay attention to your self-talk. Be conscious of what words you use to describe yourself, your actions, and the situations you are in. You can start implementing this positive practice every day and with as many people as you can.

Be particularly mindful of how you are relating to current situations. Here is what I mean.

For example, you are out on a date with your husband or friend. When you hear yourself say, "I should be working on that report," say instead, "I'm glad that I have the opportunity to spend time nurturing this relationship."

When you have noticed you haven't called your mom in a while. Instead of saying, "a good daughter would phone her mother every day," say, "I'm glad I'm able to check in on my mother and respond when she really needs me."

When we start shifting our perspective to a more positive one, we become energetic instead of stressed or depleted. We feel free and loving, and our body responds with health.

This next tool is a wonderful example to figure out what you can do to improve your circumstances.

CONTROL VS. NO CONTROL

Let's face it, you have control over two things: Your own thoughts and your own behavior. Understanding where you have control or not can be empowering.

Here's an example:

You are in the office, and someone approaches you with a bit of gossip about your coworker, Kathy. The gossip includes some rather harsh remarks about something you are passionate about. You might become defensive or antagonistic toward Kathy and begin forming alliances with others who share your conviction.

But the truth of the matter is that you have no control over what Kathy values. What you can do is stay true to what matters to you but have respect for what Kathy values as well. In addition, you have the choice to NOT engage or listen to what others are saying or interpreting. You can break the conversations of others by saying, "Kathy is not here, and I have a rule to not engage in conversations about what others think or say without them present."

It's also incredibly healing and helpful to make the distinction between:
"I'm in pain vs I have pain."
"I am in love verses I have love."
"I am scared verses I have some fear."
"I am worried verses I have some concerns."

This is also the habit of not being offended. Do you look for reasons to be offended? Do you use that word a lot? "I'm so offended." Again, this is not a chastising but simple awareness of our habits that affect our health.

Another example of control might go something like this. You arrive home from work and realize that the charity organization did not pick up your donations that day as planned. Your driveway is full of unwanted items, and it is scheduled to rain that evening.

You can either: 1) fuss and fume, call the charity office, and leave a scathing message. Or 2) you can recognize that there was a mishap with the schedule and call to ask when they can come to collect your donations. Should you cover up the items and leave them on your driveway or take them back into your garage? You really have no control over their scheduling mistake. But you do have control over your response.

The question to ask yourself is this, "Do I have any control over this situation? If I do, what rational steps can I take to resolve it? If not, am I willing to let it go?"

THE THREE QUESTIONS

There are three questions I use to turn my clients' negative thinking or feeling stuck around. I ask these questions of myself and my family and whoever happens to be visiting for dinner.

I ask these three questions because they help us to focus on the good things that are going right in our life.

So, the first question is, "What's the nicest thing that you did for somebody today or this week? It can be simple. It doesn't have to be: "I built a house for my neighbor, or I donated a million dollars." It can be as simple as, "I opened the door for strangers that had their arms full," or "I picked up a pencil for somebody at work." Small little detail things. It doesn't have to be big. So, number one, what's the nicest thing that you did for somebody?

The second question is, "What's the nicest thing that somebody did for you?"

Maybe somebody held the door open for you, or a coworker fixed you a cup of coffee, or your boss told you what a great job you did on a project that wasn't even yours. Who assisted you, thought about you, smiled at you? This can be someone you know or a complete stranger. Often it is from those we know. It is amazing how much kindness we find in others when we start searching for it.

And the third is "What's the nicest thing that you did for yourself? So often, we are so busy, particularly mothers, doing things for other people, which is not necessarily bad or wrong. That's my role, that's what I do. I'm an author, teacher, and I'm a health and wellness coach too. My whole day is about giving to other people like you. So, you need to stop every single day and take a moment and do something nice just for you. Not because somebody wants you to do it, not because you think it's good for you necessarily, but something you want. Something that you enjoy, and it doesn't have to be big.

The nicest thing I usually do for myself is to take a bath. A bath is very relaxing for me. It's a very nice cooling-off period for me. It's one of the few times in my day that I am completely alone and really take a few moments and just fully relax.

So, the three questions: The nicest thing you did for somebody, the nicest thing that somebody did for you, and the nicest thing you did for yourself. I want you to go ahead and take a moment and answer those questions right now.

It may take a moment to come up with the answers, but you can do it. It may be difficult for you because we are not used to looking for positive behaviors from ourselves and others. I am absolutely certain you are serving others, being served, and serving yourself!

If you would like to share your answers, you can go post on my BolsterUp Facebook page.

BE CURIOUS/REFRAMING

Curious George had it right. Curiosity curates happiness and health. Asking questions like, "I wonder how I could accomplish this." Or "What haven't I tried?"

There is no limit to how we can reframe and be curious. Here are some examples.

I bet a lot of people might feel this way in the same situation. I wonder who would feel differently in the same situation.
What are the benefits of my circumstance?
My favorite: What is the worse thing about this? What is the best?
What's funny about it? What is surprising?

Come up with your reframes and curious questions. It will open up a whole new world and you never know what you will discover, accomplish, or create. It's so much fun!

OUTSMARTING NEGATIVE THINKING PATTERNS

Often in our thinking, we get caught up in finger-pointing and wanting to say, "but they're not doing…" Or "but she did this to me." What's worse is that we get caught up in our past experiences that are not around us anymore. We are thinking of negative results of past relationships or a job we didn't get.

We start to victimize ourselves and make ourselves suffer, and we don't need to do that. One of the most beneficial things you can do to shift your focus to a more positive one is to start accepting people for who and what they are and not try to change them. You can also start doing the same thing for yourself.

You should not beat yourself up when you make missteps. I don't like to say mistakes because you're here to learn, you're here to practice. So, every time you think you made a mistake, remind yourself, it was just a misstep, and it's normal. If you don't like something you did and you don't like the results of that thing, that's it! It is just a misstep, and it's a practice. Now you can practice something else. Start to pay attention to how your behavior makes you feel.

That's a very healthy way to look at life and to accept yourself. You're going to have missteps, you're going to start on a certain path, and you're going to get off it occasionally. So what? Big deal, everybody does!

Love yourself! Appreciate the fact that you got off the path. Maybe you did something beautiful because you did get off the path, and you are starting a new one. Just be kind to yourself. We are here to experience joy and freedom and pleasure.

My question is, what are you doing to experience freedom, pleasure, and joy in your life?

Action Step: Get a piece of paper and a pen. I like to use a notebook to go back and remind myself of my progress! Seeing where you have been and where you are now is a great tool in and of itself!

If you are stuck on problem solving and finding it difficult to shift your perspective from any of the above techniques and practices, try this.

On the paper, write down what you think is "wrong," or what you're afraid of, or what currently has you upset. Now we are going to adopt the practice used by Sakichi Toyoda, the father of the Toyota Production System. It is called the five "WHYS."

Like a young precocious child, you ask yourself "why" five times, digging deeper and deeper into the root cause of your problem. Try to stay with the facts only. The idea is that it usually only takes five why questions to get to the bottom of a problem or negative feeling. You may need to ask a few more times, and sometimes a solution or a better feeling emerges before the five whys.

For Example: I'm stressed and feel overwhelmed because I missed a deadline for a project.

Why am I feeling stressed and overwhelmed? Because I can't find the files I need easily to do my job.

Why? The filing system is disorganized, and I have files in several different locations.

Why? Because I haven't put them all in one place.

Why? I have not made putting the files in one place a priority

Why? I didn't think it was important until now.

Conclusion: If I take the time and put the files in one place and organize them, I can get my work done more quickly and efficiently, providing me with peace and calm.

It is always best to write down what you find as the answer, and if it involves taking action, then commit to doing that. If you have a hard time setting and keeping goals, I have developed specific programs to help you get on track and stay motivated. You can find out more on my website at BolsterUp.com

THINKING CONCLUSION

> *"The world as we have created it is a process of our thinking. It cannot be changed without changing our thinking."*
> - Albert Einstein

Unhealthy thinking habits make you feel out of control, hopeless, and uncertain. Good thinking understands that there's a solution to your problems or ways around obstacles that you face.

You have learned and been open to a great deal in this first pillar of being a Happy Healthy Human. Hopefully you are committed to some mindfulness practices, particularly to a formal meditation. My recommendation is 15 minutes a day at least. I encourage you to use apps, free resources like YouTube or join me for my group coaching that includes weekly meditations.

The three questions: What is the nicest thing you did for somebody today? Second, what is the nicest thing that somebody did for you? Third, what is the nicest thing that you did for yourself?

So, the questions start to focus your attention on all the wonderful things that are a part of your life every day. I know you're already doing nice things for people; you're just not focused on it. Every little thing matters, for them and for you.

For more detailed and "prescriptive" techniques to change our thinking habits, I recommend at least fifteen minutes of meditation, writing down at least five things you are grateful for, and keeping track of the three nicest things.

For more in-depth mind shifts, I use Emotional Freedom Technique (EFT) or Process Healing with the BolsterUp Method for Emotional Healing. You can find out more at www.BolsterUp.com. One of the fastest ways to get a hold of our thinking is with our breathing. Next, we explore how breathing benefits your health, happiness, and overall well-being. One of the keys to being mindful about our thinking actually involves our breathing.

Action Step: What are one or two things you can do to implement what you learned? What obstacles can get in your way? How will you overcome them?

CHAPTER 4

PILLAR II: BREATHING

> *"Deep breathing brings deep thinking and shallow breathing brings shallow thinking."*
> - **Elsie Lincoln Benedict**

The second pillar of the Happy Healthy Human is BREATHING. We got this right as soon as we were born! Babies breathe properly. Good breathing habits are definitely tied to our well-being and support Pillar #1 our thinking. Many of us unconsciously hold our breath and this contributes to loss of good oxygenation. A proper breathing technique is essential to good blood circulation, immune function, our digestive, muscular, and nervous system function as well. In fact, our mood, health, happiness and entire life is linked to our breathing. I also want to draw your attention to *what* you are breathing. Air quality is important too.

When breathing properly, we are able to release waste and toxins, allowing our bodies to heal, and of course, inviting in the elixir of life...oxygen. In this section we will focus on good breathing habits, how to participate and how different breathing habits and techniques can change your life.

All of us are breathing if we're alive, correct? I never could quite understand when I was younger and took a lot of aerobics classes that the instructor would often say, "Don't forget to breathe." I would be thinking, "Of course I'm breathing, or I wouldn't be bouncing around in this aerobics room." But what she really meant was make sure that I'm breathing deeply, that I'm breathing regularly, and I'm taking a deep enough breath, oxygenating my body. What we have found out, and I'm sure you've heard, is most of us walk around and we're just breathing with the top third of our lungs; if you place your hands on your chest and you just breathe normally, like you normally do, walking around breathing, you will notice that it all appears at the top. All your breath is moving in and out at the top of your lungs, which is not the best way to breathe.

We need to be breathing into the lower part of the lungs. So, in order to do that you have to be deliberate about the breath you're taking until you get used to it. Babies automatically do this and I'm sure you have seen them. Sleeping beautiful little babies, their bellies rise and fall. Somehow through the mix of growing up we grew busy, the majority of us stop breathing that way and we start breathing with just the top of the lungs.

It is not beneficial to our health. It's certainly not beneficial to your gastrointestinal system for digesting food which we'll move into next when we'll talk about nourishment.

Secondly, most of us are not breathing properly. We might be taking in enough air to not fall over dead, but we are not inhaling and exhaling the way our bodies were designed. Not breathing properly has a huge effect on your health. I will teach you how to take a proper breath and which tools to use, and breathing techniques that allow more health and happiness.

YOUR NOSE IS FOR BREATHING

Let's talk about your nose. That hunk of clay, or little button or beak sitting in the middle of your face. Whatever shape it is, I want you to befriend your nose. I don't care what the shape is. It's perfect just the way it is. Your nose is an ally. It's one of your favorite new friends.

Why is your nose your ally? You need to be breathing through your nose. If you're a mouth breather you're going to have to retrain your nasal cavity to draw in air. Remember, your nose is for breathing. Your mouth is for eating. Nose is for breathing; mouth is for eating.

Why is it so important to breathe through your nose? Well, it's the first line of defense or one of the first lines of defense for your body. When you breathe through your nose, it naturally filters the air. It warms the air if it's cold, so it's better received in your lungs, and it moistens the air if it's dry. Your nose is very important to the breathing cycle. Breathing is so important to your health and your happiness. Breathing through your mouth contributes to bad breath, changes in heart rate, blood pressure, fatigue, shoulder and neck pain. In fact, bad breathing habits have been linked to increased stress hormones like cortisol that contribute to poor mood, weight gain, and not sleeping well. We already covered the science of high cortisol. This stress hormone shuts down your prefrontal cortex as well, keeping us from focus, planning, and impulse control. Our breathing, or habit of how we breathe, really stacks up.

So why are so many of us not breathing beneficially and what can we do about it? The main reason so many don't breathe beneficially is our sedentary lifestyle. Sitting with poor posture in fact. We need upright, standing posture to allow the diaphragm as well as supporting rib muscles, (called intercostal muscles), to pull air down into the lungs

We also need to let go of trying to hold our "abs" in to look thinner. However, most of us are slouching while we are sitting so this is less common. Breathing by using the muscle designed for breathing, the diaphragm, is super important. In fact, the diaphragm is the only muscle no mammal can live without. "Shallow breathing doesn't just make stress a response, it makes stress a habit for our bodies, and therefore, our minds, are locked into," says John Luckovich, an Integrative Breathwork facilitator in Brooklyn, New York.

How many of us have had a cold before and had to breathe through our mouths? It gets dry and irritating, it's gross, and it also creates bad breath. People who are mouth breathers are sicker, have lower cognitive functioning, and poor teeth. I mean, that's important. Your nose is there for a reason, let's use it. Breathe through your nose.

If you find you need help retraining your nose for breathing, Patrick McKeown writes in *The Oxygen Advantage* to tape your mouth shut! Yes, it's that important. This is not meant to offend anyone, only to highlight the degree of importance our breathing has on our wellbeing.

One of the first things any first responder does with a person, unconscious or not is assess the breathing. This should be our go to any time we are feeling anxious, nervous, fearful, or unfocused. Ask yourself, "How am I breathing?" With just a few adjustments of deliberately drawing air in and down you can calm yourself, decrease the flight or fight response and focus on what you need or want.

As soon as I have a client that reports having anxiety, we focus on a breathing protocol. I had a self-reported "very busy and stressed out" executive client. He really didn't think talking to a well-being coach was going to "solve" any of his problems. Neither did I, but I did know if he would participate for just 6 weeks and try some of the tools I could provide he would at least feel better. When we concluded our coaching a year later, he revealed to me how essential breathing was to an overall new level of happiness and peace.

So, we're going to start utilizing that cute little thing on your face, and the very useful muscle, your diaphragm. If you're not used to using your nose or diaphragm to draw in breath, it may take a couple of days to retrain your nasal cavity and breathing muscles. Warning, it can even be uncomfortable, but keep reading and I'll walk you through it.

AIR QUALITY

What you are breathing is just as important as how you are breathing. Indoor Air Quality (IAQ) is a concern in our modern industrialized world with airtight buildings to keep heating and cooling bills down, pressed wood products, carpeting, air fresheners, perfumes, and a host of pollutants we don't even consider. Indoor Air Quality refers to the air quality within and around buildings and structures, especially as it relates to the health and comfort of building occupants. Most of us understand the poor air quality from smoking but are not aware of the contributions to air quality from cleaning products, personal care products, and appliances. For instance, an improperly adjusted gas stove can emit significantly more carbon monoxide than one that is properly adjusted. There are immediate and long-term effects of poor IAQ.

It is often the total sum of these air quality contributors that create ill health, respiratory diseases, heart disease and even cancer. One way to "off gas" or allow the indoor spaces to "breathe" is to ventilate. Ventilation allows air exchange from indoor to outdoor. However, it is not practical to allow as little air exchange as possible... double pane windows, caulking, "air tight" foam insulation...no air leaks seems to be a good thing. However, if too little air exchange is available indoor air pollutants build up.

I think about this and how I got constant headaches and suffered from incredible sinus issues when I started high school. The school building had no windows. None. We relied solely on the installed ventilation system to bring in fresh air.

Let's explore some things you can do to improve your IAQ. Be familiar with volatile organic compounds and reduce them as much as possible. Volatile organic compounds (VOCs) are emitted as gases from certain solids or liquids. For starters be picky about what candles you buy and burn and other "air fresheners" you spray or plug in. Open your windows as much as possible to allow for good air exchange. Take your shoes off as soon as you walk in the door, so you don't drag outdoor pollutants in. Have your appliances checked for proper settings and ventilation. And reduce wall to wall carpeting. I am also careful of the amount of formaldehyde in my furnishings.

Reducing VOC's can improve your indoor air quality and promote healthy breathing. Consider the following:

SOURCES OF VOCS

Household products, including:

- paints, paint strippers and other solvents
- wood preservatives
- aerosol sprays
- cleansers and disinfectants
- moth repellents and air fresheners
- stored fuels and automotive products
- hobby supplies
- dry-cleaned clothing
- pesticide

Other products, including:

- building materials and furnishings
- office equipment such as copiers and printers, correction fluids and carbonless copy paper
- graphics and craft materials including glues and adhesives, permanent markers and photographic solutions

REAL LIFE STORY

I recently learned how to scuba dive. This is definitely an activity focused on breathing, proper breathing, taking breathing breaks. Not following proper breathing protocols could kill you.

Still, I was excited about adding to my exploration landscape and being able to witness what lies beneath the surface of the gorgeous waters I have often found myself in. The first couple of lessons for the scuba diving certification were fine... it was all book work. Learning about buoyancy, how to calculate PSI, atmospheres of absolute pressures, and other dive terminology. Even the initial instruction on mask clearing, controlled descent, and water entrance techniques were all fine with me. There were others in my scuba diving class that were having a difficult time putting their face in the water with their masks on and relying on the breathing apparatus.

My first qualification dive went well, at least for the first half. I thought I had a good handle on how to clear properly as my descent seemed to go well as we reached thirty feet. However, I still had some significant pressure in my left ear and continued to try to clear it. Big rookie mistake! I had to scratch the rest of my dive certification to give my bleeding ear a bit of time to heal. Six weeks later, I was back in the water, at a new quarry, and eager to receive my initial diving certification. The entrance, clearing, and descent all went well. I removed my mask, cleared it, and then all of a sudden was filled with an intense and overwhelming fear and need to be on the surface breathing through my own nose. I wanted to ascend NOW. I gave the signal to end the dive and go up. My instructor, who knew me pretty well by then, gave me instructions to breathe evenly and slowly. I shook my head no, and again, with more need and enthusiasm to go up. I felt like I needed air. I was already suffocating and was starting to hyperventilate. Hyperventilating is a real issue for divers. Rapid breathing sucks up limited oxygen supplies, decreases CO_2 blood levels, can increase heart rate, and make you light-headed. I couldn't do it. I needed to breathe on my own. Again, he held his hands up, knowing this is how divers get hurt. I really wanted to push off the bottom and get to the surface as fast as I could. I was only about 30 feet down, but I knew there was still a need to control the ascent.

I was working against myself with my rapid breathing. My sympathetic nervous system was flooding my body with flight neurotransmitters due to the signal of my rapid shallow breathing. Our breathing has a tremendous influence on the release of hormones in our bodies.

I did as instructed and forced myself to concentrate on my diaphragm and push air continuously out and slowly inhale air back in. Control the breath, deliberate exertion on the out-breath, and slow even inhale.

I started to feel less panic by *not* sucking on my regulator. I was breathing more normally and feeling much better and more comfortable. I just hung on the bottom for about two minutes, just a few slow breaths. Like magic, the panic subsided, I felt clear-headed and finished my testing. I had never in my life felt so out of control, so reliant on equipment to sustain my life, and the intense feeling of suffocating. Panic attacks occur on land in people all the time. I now understood this intense, horrifying experience.

However, it was the breathing that made the difference in my panic or my calm. Rapid breathing only increased the panic and feeling like I needed more air. I have been practicing and sharing the benefits of different breathing techniques for stress and anxiety reduction for years in my practice, but never had I experienced the immediate situation change a few controlled breaths could provide. Let's look at the science behind breathing and what was happening during my panic state versus my calm state, and why proper breaths make all the difference.

DETAILED SCIENTIFIC EVIDENCE

There is a science to everything from intricate, sophisticated systems like rockets to simpler daily occurrences like cooking and cleaning that we don't spend too much time thinking about. I love science. It is everywhere and part of everything. So, what happens when we are not getting the right intake and output of O_2 and CO_2? When we find ourselves in panic mode, like my scuba diving experience, our breathing is rapid and shallow, and too much carbon dioxide is released. Not having an adequate balance of carbon dioxide leads to that feeling of suffocation, often accompanied by dizziness and numbness. More breathing, or rapid breathing, isn't really a good fix here. It is a pause in air intake that allows the carbon dioxide levels to come back up and dissipate the feeling of needing more air.

Therefore, it is often suggested for those hyperventilating to breathe into a paper bag, rebreathing the expelled air forces more carbon dioxide back into the mix, restoring proper CO_2. Balance seems to be the key. Not too much in or out for a state of calm and peace. My scuba diving instructor could see I was taking in too much air too fast, and by forcing a controlled exhale, and slow exhale it would restore the balance needed.

It's actually cool to think about how easily we can alter the chemistry in our body just by adjusting our breathing! There is more to learn at BolsterUp.com

There is much more to breathing than just deescalating a panic attack. Just as the chemical mix needed to be just right to keep me on the bottom of the quarry to finish my scuba diving lessons. Breathing also affects other chemicals in our bodies. Noradrenaline has been getting a lot of attention in neuropsychological research. How we choose to breathe makes a tremendous difference in the chemicals produced in our brain and can either enhance or diminish our health, happiness, and humanity.

It seems the major connection to breathing and well-being is tied to the vagus nerve. "Vagus" is Latin, meaning wandering. The vagus nerve, also referred to as the X or 10th cranial nerve, is a long, complex nerve that connects the brain to the abdomen. It runs through the face, down the neck, and branches out, or wanders, to other critical areas of our body and ends at the colon. The vagus nerve is the most important and longest nerve of the 12 cranial nerves responsible for regulating heart rate, blood pressure, digestion, sweating, speaking, and of course, breathing. Some cranial nerves are responsible for sensory information, and other cranial nerves control movement, and some special ones do both, like the vagus nerve. How well your vagus nerve functions is referred to as vagal tone. Chronic stress can decrease your vagal tone and leads to anxiety, inflammation, digestive issues, and other health problems.

We can stimulate the vagus nerve with abdominal breathing or holding our breath. When stimulated with deliberate deep breaths, the vagus nerve signals the heart to pump slower, decreasing blood pressure and eliciting a state of calm. This is why the 4 7 8 breathing technique and other diaphragmatic breathing work so well to decrease stress, anxiety and create overall relaxation, and it is my go-to. I'll teach you about this in the practice section.

The big player for all the benefits of abdominal breathing that stimulates the vagus nerve is secretion of the influential neurotransmitter acetylcholine. Acetylcholine is the MVP of neurobiology. Acetylcholine is a critical parasympathetic neurotransmitter stimulating the "rest and digest" response and affects the "fight or flight response." Breathing improperly can alter the release and function of acetylcholine resulting in significant problems with memory and movement. See why breathing and this MVP neurotransmitter is so important? Are you already sitting up straighter and using your diaphragm to take in a nice slow long deep breath?

Trinity College Institute of Neuroscience and the Global Brain Health Institute at Trinity found that participants who focused well while undertaking a task that demanded a lot of attention had greater synchronization between their breathing patterns and their attention than those who had poor focus. Ancient Eastern teachings have been connecting breath to the state of mind and body for thousands of years. This is not new information.

Other researchers are looking at breathing and different diseases like Alzheimer's. Sleep-Disordered Breathing (SDB) appears to be associated with biological signs of Alzheimer's disease in older adults, but it is not known whether SDB causes these changes or if Alzheimer's tissue damage causes SDB (Ricardo S. Osorio, MD).

Author of *The Oxygen Advantage*, Patrick McKeown, reveals fascinating information about the relationship breathing has with our health. He goes over the research of prominent Russian physician Dr. Konstantin's breathing intervention, Buteyko, and the concept of over-breathing. Konstantin Pavlovich Buteyko was the creator of the Buteyko method for the treatment of asthma and other breathing disorders. My big takeaway from the research and practical protocols outlined in the book is always to breathe through your nose, and work to improve your body's oxygenation. The Buteyko, known in Russia as Voluntary Elimination of Deep Breathing or VEDB, was used to treat asthma patients as well as improve oxygenation of cardiac patients. Many physicians and chest physiotherapists teach the Buteyko method, or as Patrick McKeown has applied the method through his BOLT (Body Oxygen Level Test) score improvement practices. Athletes flock to McKeown's teachings, as do the regular couch potatoes, asthmatics, and other folks with compromised breathing to improve overall health and stamina.

What science, research, and ancient wisdom tell us is controlled, less frequent breathing is essential for health and happiness. What I learned from McKeown that was most valuable, and a bit contradictory to what we all hear, is holding a breath can be more valuable than trying to take another deep breath.

One of the reasons drawing air in through the nose is so important is when air passes over the mucus membrane it produces nitric oxide in our sinuses. Breathing through your nose conditions the air and filters it. Mouth breathing does none of this. Mouth breathing can also cause fatigue due to the lack of oxygenation. There are a host of reasons to breathe through your nose. It's not an accident a nose is part of our anatomy!

LET IT BREATH

> *"Breath is the bridge which connects life to consciousness, which unites your body to your thoughts."*
> - **Thich Nhat Hanh**

A mounting body of research is supporting the notion of letting relationships, projects, and ideas breathe too. (https://www. ncbi.nlm.nih.gov/pmc/articles/PMC6843288/) I teach a few techniques that support this idea improving productivity, overall well-being, and brain health. The Pomodoro Technique has been in my coaching tool kit for many years, and it is easy to participate in and has the benefits of scheduled breaks. The premise is that our focus, attention and brain is like a small child, if they know there is playtime coming, will do a better job to focus on a task for a specified period. However, you must allow the breaks when you say you are going to provide them, we can't lie to children, nor can we lie to ourselves.

The Pomodoro technique involves participating in a task for a specified amount of time and then walking away, letting it breathe for a short break, then setting the timer for another session followed by another short breather. After four sessions, it is helpful for overall well-being and brain health to take a longer break or breather. The adage of forcing ourselves to push through fatigue and boredom to get something done faster is actually false. Studies show taking a breather or breaks actually improves performance, cuts down the time it takes to complete tasks, and improves information assimilation.

Over twenty years ago, my diagnosis of an autoimmune disorder was a huge wake-up call to decrease the stress in my life. I had two active toddlers, was running my own clothing manufacturing company, and dealing with major domestic emotional pain. The only deep breathing I was doing was gasping for air on my daily runs. While searching for ways to help my body with the autoimmune disorder, I kept coming across breathing exercises. I had a physician also tell me to spend some time each day doing diaphragmatic breathing or belly breathing.

All diaphragmatic breathing means is using your abdomen, more specifically your diaphragm, to pull air deep into your lungs. I was willing to try just about anything, so I sat to breathe. I took deep, deliberate breaths while standing in the grocery store line. I especially used my belly breathing when I felt angry or aggravated, like waiting, and waiting, and waiting to be called back for one of many doctor's appointments. It seemed to help, although I didn't have any understanding as to why at that time.

However, now I know why these deep breathing breaks were helping me feel more calm, peaceful and perhaps aid my body's ability to heal. Deep breathing stimulates the vagus nerve. AHH! My deep breathing exercises were deepening or opening communication between my brain and digestive system. As mentioned earlier, this special nerve is part of the parasympathetic systems aptly referred to as the "rest and digest" nervous system. Deep breathing when practiced regularly "tones" the vagus nerve. Vagal tone represents the amount of activity in this cranial nerve. Higher vagal tone means more activity in the nerve, which results in a faster relaxation response. Breathing is so vital to our health.

I credit the start of my deep breathing exercises to be the catalyst for my healing. Deep deliberate breaths through my nose not only created a sense of calm but it was helping to oxygenate my body properly. I ran and exercised a lot and often ended up with a migraine. One theory was that I became hypoxic. Mostly, when we are exercising heavily, we open our mouths to draw in more air. However, this was working against me. When I started to force myself to get my oxygen through only my nose, my headaches disappeared. It was a process, and it took me about a month of deliberate nose breathing work, as outlined in *Oxygen Advantage*, to get through a run without opening my mouth. If I can do it, so can you. And it is so worth the added mindfulness of keeping your mouth closed. Plus, no bugs or flies got in my teeth while galloping through the woods.

I had a client who is a prominent business owner, and he purchased a wellness program for all his employees. Although he has his own on-call medical staff, he wanted to set a good example by participating in a few coaching calls but had no real need for coaching. I was his coach. He let me know at the opening of our first session that he had all the medical experts he could wish for, and no offense to me, but he couldn't really think of anything I might offer to improve his health. Not being discouraged, I led him through my coaching regime. We ended up focusing on breathing, and he reported to me the tremendous difference the practices I was encouraging him to participate in were having in his life. I ended up being his coach for over a year until his company switched wellness providers (he was shocked to learn I didn't come with the new insurance company his company was switching to). This is what he had to say.

I just want to thank you personally for all your excellent guidance which has truly helped improve my health. You are an outstanding professional and your efforts have changed my perceptions about the value of health coaches. I will miss our calls but will always be grateful for your interest and coaching. A better gift, I could never have received. Best always to you. I'll always remember you when I practice my breathing exercises!

I had another client who was having difficulty passing company-wide exams due to anxiety. I had her practice the 4-7-8 breathing Dr. Weil promotes. She reported being less anxious and more able to focus during her tests and started to improve her performance. She passed her exam and got promoted. Yes, breathing can definitely change your life in more ways than one.

My children also use deep breathing to help control their emotions. Being a teenager in high school can be challenging. My oldest daughter called me one day after school to help lead her friend through a breathing exercise. Her friend was deeply troubled and crying uncontrollably over a scholarship she did not receive. She listened to my directions, and we went through four cycles of the 4 7 8 breathing together. She reported feeling much better, stopped crying, and was able to talk to me about other options to pay for college.

Breathing has a tremendous influence on our lives. Focused breathing and breaks keep our bodies, relationships, and ideas healthy and happy.

PRACTICE TO APPLY FOR NOW

TAKING A PROPER BREATH

In this section, I'm going to teach you how to breathe properly. I also provide different breathing techniques you can try for different effects like to focus, energize, or create calm and relaxation. Breathing exercises can make the lungs function more efficiently and are recommended for everyone. Top notch athletes, and teachers, doctors, lawyers (especially lawyers!), accountants, moms, dads, children, all benefit from breathing exercises. In fact, those with compromised pulmonary function like people with COPD and asthma, breathing exercises help to keep the lungs strong.

Let's learn how to take a proper breath. First, I'd like for you to lay down with your knees bent and your hands by your side. If you have a piece of paper or a light magazine, get it before you lay down. Next, place the paper or the magazine on your belly. With your knees bent, hands by your side, take in a breath. I want you to really concentrate on moving that paper. Think about your muscles down there, your diaphragm, and pull air in. As you pull the air in, the paper should rise. Then push the air out and let the paper fall.

I will tell you that if you're not used to breathing properly, this muscle needs to be built back up. Practice this breathing technique for three minutes twice a day. I know that we've been breathing since we were born, but this kind of breathing is different. It's a kind of breathing that is beneficial and healthier, and what we all did as babies!

I can tell you that the more you practice these deep breaths, the more your diaphragm gets used to being used and the easier it is for you to breathe. In my experience, when I started doing this, it did not feel very good, it kind of hurt.

I want you to take three or four deep breaths, really concentrate on trying to find that diaphragm, and move that paper. Again, if it's uncomfortable, it will ease as you start doing this a couple of times throughout the day or on a more regular consistent basis. Just do it as part of your morning and evening routine or as part of your exercise.

After you get used to doing this laying down, stand up and try to do the same thing. Obviously, you're not going to use the paper while standing but you can use your hand. It's going to be a little bit more difficult. Think about that diaphragm, and this time, you're going to try to move your hand. Breathe in a relaxing way down in your abdomen, using your diaphragm to draw in air and push air out.

Also, while doing this exercise, do not suck in your stomach so you look thinner. It is important to allow the air to fill your lungs which expands your belly. A lot of us walk around trying to look thin by sucking in our stomachs. But we're really cutting off good circulation and proper breathing techniques by doing that. Some experts believe that by following good breathing techniques you tighten and flatten your abs. Easy, relaxed breathing using your diaphragm is correct breathing.

BREATHING TECHNIQUES

THE 4-7-8 BREATHING TECHNIQUE

This breathing technique is one of my absolute favorites. I teach it to everybody; I teach it to kids, and I teach it to parents, Navy SEALS, factory workers and CEOs. I want everybody to start practicing this breathing technique. It is one of the fastest ways to rid your body and your mind of an anxious state, invite calm, peace and relaxation. If you have depression or you're stressed, this is a very fast and simple technique that you can start implementing today.

It's called the 4-7-8 breathing technique. The 4 stands for the amount of time that you're going to breathe in, 7 is how long you're going to hold your breath, and you're going to exhale for 8. You're going to do that for four rounds. Remember to breathe in through your nose for the count of four, hold it for seven, and then exhale for eight. Are you ready? Let's try that together. Stand up nice and tall or sit or even lay down. The beauty of this 4-7-8 breathing technique is that you can do it anywhere. But don't do this while you're driving or operating heavy machinery because it is very relaxing.

Here we go; first, we're going to get rid of all the air that's in our lungs with a big exhale. Now in for four, hold for seven, and out for eight. If you want to kick it up a notch, I suggest that you hold your tongue on the back of your teeth between your upper gum line and your teeth.

Anyone familiar with yoga may already know how to do this. It's one of the little extra things you can do to maximize the benefits of this breathing technique. Now again, you're going to do this for four rounds. It really takes minutes (actually only one minute and 3 seconds!).

I encourage you to do this twice a day. And you know the best times to do it? When you're already doing your thinking before you go to bed at night and when your head is resting on that pillow; do four rounds of the 4-7-8 breathing.

Doing this breathing technique as you go to sleep helps your body naturally heal. You naturally find a state of health and happiness. It's best to practice 4-7-8 breathing, twice a day at least, but don't do more than four rounds. I assure you that after implementing this more often, you will achieve the proper breathing habit, and your body will benefit quickly.

NADI SHODHANA ("THE SWEET BREATH")

Alternate Nostril Breathing is best for when you need to focus or increase energy. This is not a bedtime or relaxation breathing technique.

Hold your right hand up and curl your index and middle finger toward your palm. Place your thumb next to your right nostril and your ring finger and pinky by your left. Close the right nostril by pressing gently against it with your thumb and inhale through the left nostril. The breath should be slow, steady and full. Alternate for 10 cycles.

BI-LATERAL BREATHING

This technique can be done anytime, any place. This technique is especially effective before bed, to help with sleeping.

To start, push all the air out of your lungs with an exhale. Then inhale for a count of four, and then exhale for a count of four — all through the nose. Do as many rounds as you would like.

BOX BREATHING

This is best for heightening performance and concentration and a potent stress reliever.

This technique is similar to box breathing or Sama Vritti but like a box, or square, you breathe in, hold, breath out and hold for the same count. Start with 4 but you can choose a higher number.

BREATHING CONCLUSION

Breathing is so important to our quality of life and the effectiveness of our lives. The ability to harness your breath is one of the most important and least taught areas of health, happiness, and well-being.

Breathing is a sign of life. It's automatic, and most of us don't spend too much time thinking about breathing unless it becomes difficult, like when you have a stuffed-up nose. It is important to breathe through your nose. Your nose filters and conditions the air as it comes into your body. Mouth breathing exposes you to more pathogens, dries out your mouth, and causes unnecessary health concerns.

There are many health benefits of breathing through the vessel that was designed to bring air into our bodies. In addition to keeping us alive, there is much we can do for our health, happiness, and well-being by being deliberate and mindful about breathing. Deep breathing exercises decrease stress, create an immediate sense of calm, and help us to focus.

We often take our breathing for granted. Because breathing is automatic, we don't spend much time thinking about the ways we can alter our breath for better health and happiness. Breathing is free, and by being deliberate about how we are breathing, it can make a huge difference in every area of our lives. Our breathing has a direct link to the hormones or neurotransmitters released and surging throughout our biological system. We can't be in a panicked or flight or frightened state and a calm, peaceful, mindful state at the same time. Our breathing can decrease the amount of stress we experience in our lives. The more we can decrease stress, the healthier, happier, and more human we become.

Different types of breathing can give athletes the added advantage, as well as decrease or eliminate disease and illness. Proper nose breathing, especially as a child, forms the contours of the face and can have a major impact on learning and behavior. The good news, even if nose breathing is challenging because of habit, current medical conditions, or just that it is hard, like when exercising, it can be improved.

I encourage you to spend a few moments a day deliberately focused on controlling your breathing. Other breathing techniques can warm up a cold body or cool down a hot body. Deliberate, controlled breathing can, in fact, save your life. At the very least, focusing on your breathing will improve your overall well-being.

Some common areas to let breathe:

- Body...don't wear undies to bed
- House... open windows, have good plants, decrease indoor air
- pollution...candles, sprays, cleaning supplies
- Plants, relationships, kids...give them space to breathe.

The nose really is for breathing and the mouth for eating, which brings us to the third pillar, Nourishment.

Action Step: What are one or two things you can do to implement what you learned? What obstacles can get in your way? How will you overcome them?

CHAPTER 5

PILLAR III: NOURISHMENT

Nourish - "provide with the food or other substances necessary for growth, health, and good condition and keep (a feeling or belief) in one's mind, typically for a long time."

The third pillar in the BolsterUp program to be a happy, healthy human is your nourishment. The first pillar is thinking. Your head sits on top, so it's number one. Your breathing comes next, and then third is nourishment. Like our thinking and breathing, this nourish pillar is far more than just what you are eating. We nourish our bodies, yes, and nourishment is vital for health and may not be what you currently think nourishing is. However, it is also vital to nourish our ideas, relationships, and projects.

Nourishment is important for proper development; it's necessary for health and good condition. When you are a properly nourished person, you become more active and positive throughout the day. Proper nutrition is one of the factors that will assist your body in healing as well as participating in activities of life. Of course, you know this. I want to discuss with you what exactly nourishing is for you as a bio-individual.

Eating and absorbing nutrients are two different things. Many people eat a lot but are malnourished for various reasons. If your body is already trying very hard to deal with a high amount of inflammation or need for repair, some foods may not be readily used by your body even if they are healthy foods. For example, those with celiac disease, or colitis, pancreatic insufficiency, or a number of autoimmune disorders simply can't digest at the right level to absorb the nutrients. Trust me. Been there and done that! So, for the sake of argument, healthy does not necessarily mean nourishing! And the word or label "food" certainly does not guarantee it is nourishment. Oreo's anyone, Cheeto's?

There are many people who are not properly nourished, particularly if they are ill. I am not even referring to underdeveloped countries or impoverished neighborhoods. I'm talking about those that eat enough food but are still lacking in the ingredients to allow their body to heal, function and be in health.

Improper nourishment or digestion can result from three major things:

- eating the wrong kinds of food

- eating too quickly

- digestive abuse

All three of these can result in undigested food rotting, fermenting and going rancid in your digestive system, nutrients not being absorbed and improper weight.

Nourishment is important for proper development; it's necessary for health and good condition. When you are a properly nourished person, you become more active and positive throughout the day. This kind of behavior is good, especially if you are a busy or sick person. Eating unconsciously will make you less healthy, and it affects your happiness and human experience.

We are not the same when it comes to diets. We are all unique individuals. We are bio-individuals subject to our thinking, breathing, behavior patterns, and environment. What works for me for nourishment won't necessarily work for you. Our nourishment requirements change with time, life circumstance, and activity level. Different strokes for different folks is definitely true here, but also true that different strokes for the same folks depending on other factors.

My philosophy about food, as well as key insights I help my clients understand, helps them unlock their potential and creates a healthy, happy, human who likes the body they live in. That's why there are so many different diets that really work for one person that won't work for another. There are some basics we all need. I always start any "weight loss" (more on this term later) with the most overlooked essential nourishment. Water!

Nourishing our relationships, ideas, and projects improves our overall well-being and happiness. We nourish our bodies with real foods. We nourish our ideas and relationships by what we choose to place our attention on. For example, are we choosing to come home from work and pour a drink or leash the dog and go for a walk? Are we choosing to invite our children to play a game outside in the fresh air or to "veg" on the couch? We can nourish our relationships by being deliberate about what we "feed" them. Simple texts throughout the day or a handwritten note in a lunch box can do a lot of heavy lifting toward nourishing our relationships. Hugs are nourishing as well. When we are involved in loving gestures or just witness them, we nourish ourselves and our relationships by releasing good feelings and hormones like oxytocin. It is also important to understand when our relationships are "sick," our biological bodies have a difficult time staying healthy even with proper nutrition. Nourishment is so much more encompassing than just eating your greens or going organic!

REAL LIFE STORY

I had what started out to be an odd conversation with a client one day. She was overweight, morbidly obese as per doctors' diagnosis, and wanted to find a solution to lower her body mass. However, she was completely confused about what to eat. She had tried doing Keto, South Beach, Paleo all to no lasting change. Sure she would shed some pounds in the first few weeks, but didn't feel well and worse it was just such a pain to not have bread. During our conversation she shocked me a bit by an observation and request she made. "I noticed that some cultures seem to produce super thin people but I see them eating noodles, rice and all sorts of carbs."

I never really thought about it like that, but she made a decent point, and one I couldn't actually answer. Like I do for many clients I started to research what other cultures ate, and asked her to do the same and we could compare notes at our next meeting.

As a Health and Well-being coach I do not prescribe or treat but do on occasion, with permission from my client make recommendations. An eating plan I and many others recommend is a Mediterranean diet. And for good reason. The first being Spain has the healthiest population in the world. Although the weather in Spain is great for lots of outdoor time, walking, and the custom is to linger over mealtime. However, much of Spain's health success is attributed to their Mediterranean style of eating, and The United Nations Educational, Scientific and Cultural Organization (UNESCO) agrees. So, I was curious to find where other culture diets fit into this. I knew that a SAD (Standard American Diet) is what my client was wanting to move away from, and for good reason. The SAD eating plan is too high in saturated fat, sodium, added sugars, and calories.

It is also low in fiber traditionally gotten from eating fruits, vegetables, and whole grains.

At our next meeting she came armed with her own information and concluded a traditional Japanese diet has lots of plant-based items and seafood. It also seems to include a lot of rice and little if no wheat. Not too far from the top spot of the Mediterranean diet. And Japanese have one of the highest life expectancies. In addition to lots of plants, the Japanese consume fermented foods, and green tea. My client's conclusion was to consume a heck of a lot more vegetables, a lot less meat in all forms, and get moving a bit more. We set some goals.

As mentioned previously in this book, what started and kept me on this journey of happy health human was being diagnosed with an autoimmune disorder early in my life. My doctors were sure my condition had *nothing* to do with what I ate. Of course, this was hard to swallow since my intestines were telling a different story and I had a fast pass to die.

This was over 20 years ago now and my physicians, no matter how specialized, would not address food as nourishment or detriment to my health.

I was determined to figure out what, if anything, would be nourishing and healing to my body. I was also under a tremendous amount of stress; emotional, mental, and physical. Nothing was being nourished in my life.

I had to figure out what foods were nourishing for me. I started an in-depth search for foods that my body could handle and were nourishing. To do this I decided to go on an elimination diet.

Processed and ultra-processed food had to go. I eliminated all those for seven days, just give it a try. I went on for a full year to source only whole food.

If you need to go thirty days to figure it out, then take the time. You are worth it; you are worth figuring out your health and this is going to have a major impact on your healing and your happiness to get your nourishment down.

I started adding one type and source of food at a time. It was a pain at first but my body quickly let me know what was "nourishing" and what wasn't.

My body let me know raw vegetables were too harsh for my sore intestinal tract. But I could have steamed vegetables.

Bananas were not tolerated. Neither was red meat, bread, sugar, or corn.

I started this while raising my three children as infants to age 5. The good news was my husband was on deployment in the military, so I just had to provide nourishment for the kids. And my two older ones loved steamed broccoli! I learned not to even try a lick of ice-cream. Not so much for the milk issues but for the gluten avoidance at the time, as well as other ingredients I was eliminating. Yeah, there is gluten in lots of ice cream! Read the labels, ask at ice cream shops.

When ill, it's really important to eliminate all preservatives, all unhealthy ingredients that your body doesn't need. Eliminate all processed foods that are toxic to your body. Now when I mean all processed foods, I mean ALL processed foods. That means no store-bought dressing. That means no chicken breast that has different stuff injected into it. You also shouldn't buy vegetables in a can. Frozen is ok. Buy vegetables at a vegetable stand or at a farmer's market, and lastly, your grocery store.

When I did the elimination diet, I ate an array of vegetables (steamed not raw when I was very ill) and then I started incorporating fruit, then a little bit of chicken and rice. I know for my system that my body doesn't break down meat very well. I don't have a lot of hydrochloric acid to really break down a hunk of meat. So, when I eat meat, I usually eat chicken, or fish. It is important to pay attention to your body and learn what foods are nourishing for you in your current state of health. As your body climbs out of illness and frees itself of inflammation you will find foods that once harmed you can be eaten and tolerated. However, you first must gain a robust system of digestion back. Let's talk about how to start figuring out what foods are beneficial for you.

DETAILED SCIENTIFIC EVIDENCE

Over the centuries, much has been debated and discovered concerning diet and the nutrition derived from what we eat. I found Kenneth J. Carpenter's work, *A Short History of Nutritional Science* (March 2003), to be informative and interesting.

There has been a growing shift within the medical community over the last few decades on the relationship between diet and health. Although many identifiable health outcomes have been associated with proper nutrition or lack of specific nutrients, there has been a shift in the focus of diet on health. For example, I was told by many experts in the medical community that what I ate had no effect on the ulcerative colitis that was threatening my life. In fact, I argued with more than one gastroenterologist on this premise.

In *Special Diets for Special Kids* by Lisa Lewis, Ph.D., she talks about a study where removing an offending agent, such as dairy, restored the children's health and the recurring ear infections disappeared. However, when instructed to allow the offending agent back into the diet, the children regained ear infections.

Dr. Hass and Dr. Gottschall discovered that, when it comes to digestive disorders and other illnesses, food plays a vital role. Dr. Hass developed the Specific Carbohydrate diet for celiac disease.

In the Biochemical Aspect of Breathing (2002), Christopher Gelber addressed a 74% improvement in asthmatics using an elimination diet, not medication. Those with irritable bowel syndrome experienced a 79% significant improvement (Borok, 1994). We are what we eat. It is vital to understand what foods, deemed healthy or not, are beneficial for you.

Upwards of 12 million Americans are diagnosed with fibromyalgia mostly due to excitotoxins. Excitotoxins are substances, such as MSG and aspartate, that act as excitatory neurotransmitters, and can lead to neurotoxicity when used in excess. These neurotoxins are often used to enhance flavor by stimulating tongue receptors with no nutritional value or preservation of food. Food cravings anyone? All our favorite fast-food chains use them, yep even Chick-Fil-A. For more information you can visit TruthinLabeling.com

Neurotoxins may damage neurons, axons, and/or glia resulting in loss of specific nuclei and/or axonal tracts or demyelination. However, diets of fibromyalgia patients (albeit lots of other autoimmune diseases as well) that eliminate these offending agents have shown dramatic improvement and recovery.

I do attribute my full recovery from my own autoimmune disorder to eliminating all ultra processed, processed, and other foods that my body could not handle. It restored my health and saved my life without drugs or surgery.

There is no doubt we need to bridge current medical technology and sound practical positive habits for daily living. It is a long tradition of "conventional medicine" to debunk solid sound advice in favor of "tradition." For example, the brilliant Alexander Fleming was doing his darndest to educate army doctors that the practice of using antiseptics was killing more soldiers than helping. Another "in the know physician" agreed and went on to say for deep wounds, only a saline solution is needed to attract white blood cells and allow the body to do the rest. Sadly, these "quacks" were not given due consideration, and many men died at the hands of physicians who refused to accept something "new."

One of the biggest backlashes on the brilliance of discovering new practices that will prolong lives and not cause death by doctors was the story of Dr. Semmelweis. Ignaz Semmelweis, a Hungarian physician known as the "Savior of Mothers," made the connection of washing hands between patients. Actually, he made the connection that handling dead, diseased bodies and then immediately delivering babies was not such a great idea. We scoff at such horrifying disregard for this logic now, but back in his day, he was the one ridiculed. His insistence on medical staff to wash their hands before touching obstetric patients caused him to lose his job and later his life. The severe condemnation he received from his colleagues and the established medical society pushed him to an insane asylum, where he died just two weeks later. I find it so sad that many are still dying today because current medical practices do not accept the sound thinking of our own brilliant "quacks" of our time.

REAL LIFE STORY

As a young mother, it was devastating learning that I had a life-threatening disease. I was diagnosed with ulcerative colitis. Intestinal issues ran in my family. My great-grandmother died of colon cancer, my grandfather (her son) had a colectomy, which is the complete removal of intestines. My own mother passed away at age fifty-six. I was very aware of what could become of my life if I survived, and how quickly my life could be over. I wanted none of it.

To rule out Crohn's disease, they would need to do some more tests and blood work. Crohn's disease can skip around the whole digestive tract. However, it affects the full thickness of the bowel wall, unlike ulcerative colitis, where the rectum and large intestine lining are involved. Both are inflammation of the gastrointestinal tract blamed on our bodies' abnormal immune response. In other words, our bodies are attacking themselves.

The embarrassment of different social aspects of being sick and the countless demands of physicians were worse than the diagnosis. The last thing I needed was to be suffering and alone because I wanted to follow my instincts and stop using the medications. I just felt like there was something I could be doing to help my body do what it naturally knew how.

My doctors presented me with two long-term treatment choices. See if drug therapy worked or have surgery to remove affected areas. This would eventually lead to me having my bowels surgically removed and allowing food to pass to an artificial collection device. Knowing colon cancer ran in my family, I started with the easier of the two treatment options… drug therapy… lots and lots of drugs several times a day. Some of that required me to lay down and be still for twenty minutes after each dose. Not easy with two babies still in diapers that needed my full supervision.

One gastroenterologist finally leveled with me and told me he was under oath to only discuss and provide treatments approved by governing medical societies. Even if he knew of diet-related or lifestyle things to help, he couldn't discuss it with me. He would lose his license, so all he could offer were drugs or surgery. I was on my own to try anything else. I started to research the topic of diet and my disease in earnest. I was dedicating hours of my days to trawling the Internet, reading books, and even wading through medical journals. I quickly became an "expert." My research started to reveal there is evidence for safer alternatives to healing, including what I did and didn't eat! Some unconventional doctors a few decades ago were saying diet *does* matter. Of course, these doctors were considered quacks by the "normal" medical community, including my physicians.

I decided to do an elimination diet based on my research. Now there is quite a bit of information to backup elimination diets to help with many diseases' states and illnesses from ADHD to eczema. I'm thrilled to see much research paying attention and giving what we eat the central role in health in the past few years.

One of the latest studies I read was a review and update of the latest literature on the role of diet and inflammatory bowel disease. Dr. Oriana Damas, Luis Grace, RD, and Dr. Maria Abreu write, "Diet plays an integral role in development of inflammatory bowel disease and continues to act as a mediator of intestinal inflammation once disease sets in." A far cry from what I was told over 20 or even 12 years ago. It's not surprising my doctors, from internal medicine to specialists like gastroenterologists, didn't give much thought to diet and disease. In fact, nutrition wasn't part of the curriculum to become a physician for most medical schools.

David Eisenberg, adjunct associate professor of nutrition at Harvard T.H. Chan School of Public Health, Executive Vice President for Health Research and Education at the Samueli Institute, and founder of Healthy Kitchens/Healthy Lives, is changing all that. The international journal of Adolescent Medicine and Health tested the basic nutrition knowledge of fourth-year medical students. The results were dismal, getting more than half the questions wrong, resulting in a failing grade. (Damas, O.M., Garces, L. & Abreu, M.T. Diet as Adjunctive

Treatment for Inflammatory Bowel Disease: Review and Update of the Latest Literature. *Curr Treat Options Gastro* 17, 313–325 (2019). https://doi.org/10.1007/s11938-019-00231-8).

There is now a protocol your doctor or nutritionist can assist you with when undertaking an elimination diet. Much has been written about elimination diets, protocols, and plans for specific issues. *The Elimination Diet* by Suhani Bora MD, J. Adam Rindfleisch MPhil, MD (2018) is a good start.

I'm looking forward to more information on lifestyle medicine and nutrition being on the medical boards, so more medical school curriculums give nutrition the attention it deserves. Having physicians knowledgeable about nutrition and disease will decrease disease, drug dependency, and surgery. I don't pretend nutrition is the answer for all disease and medical needs, but it is a much bigger contributor in the last one hundred years than physicians have acknowledged. At the time of my diagnosis, the doctors and medical professionals that were saying nutrition is key were considered quacks, not unlike Dr. Semmelweis, who pushed for hand washing between patients.

As a well-being coach, I have many clients who bring mindfulness to their eating, deliberately choose whole food over processed items, and report being able to eat things like cheese again. Others have reported utilizing 30-day clean eating, like Whole 30, to revitalize their energy, mood, and creativity. I think of food now in terms of energy. Lots of fresh vegetables to me are like a clear glass. The more processed items I add to my body is like adding mud to my clean, clear glass. Even when the mud is dumped out, it leaves a residue, and I can longer see through the glass. Our diets can either leave us feeling clean and clear like the see-through glass or sluggish and dull like the muddy glass.

My clients not only report feeling physically lighter and less weighed down, but also mentally clearer. Nourishing is more than eating the right food that is beneficial for you. We nourish our dreams and goals, and interests when we have the energy to focus and be attentive.

During my auto-immune recovery, I was also learning to nourish my projects and relationships. I was experiencing severe emotional trauma in a personal relationship. I started making conscious choices to focus my attention on more sustaining, nourishing relationships at the time. This was just as important as the nourishing foods I was now providing for my health, happiness, and well-being.

PRACTICE TO APPLY NOW

I often ask myself, "What can I do today to show I care for myself tomorrow?" As well as all those things that contribute to my happiness and health. In other words, what am I currently, at this moment, doing that is for the benefit of my future self?

What can you do today to experience a better tomorrow?

The best thing you can do to nourish your body and life is to choose what you put in your mouth, and what comes out! This is not the end to nourishing well-being, but it is a start and can have a great impact on how you experience life. If you are at all interested in your well-being, getting mostly whole food is the place to start. You don't have to be perfect with this unless you are currently experiencing disease, are overweight, or feel too tired to get through your day. I currently live with an 80/20 rule since I am free of disease and usually have plenty of energy. If 80 percent of the time I am eating whole food, or organic, lots of vegetables, and water, 20 percent of the time, I can get away with having conventional treats like cookies and cake.

WATER BREAK

Water is essential for all of life. Most of us are not getting enough water and including too many beverages that work against hydration, like caffeine and alcohol. I'm not going to say no coffee or wine, but you have to do the math and make sure you are getting enough hydrating fluids. You need water to help with all stages of digestion. Water is needed for proper saliva production, which is the first stage of digestion and mastication (chewing). Stomach fluids also need adequate water, as does proper elimination functions like urinating and defecating. And this is just for digestion! Each and every cell needs some H2O too. Adequate water intake is so important for all system functions, from spinal cord insulation and good nerve function to muscle maintenance and tissue repair.

Being dehydrated is very much disliked by your brain! Often not being able to focus, feeling tired, cranky, and plain just "blah" is due to not having proper water intake.

To get a good idea of how much water you need, divide your body weight by half. Whatever half your body weight is is the number of ounces of water to shoot for.

Tip: drink a full glass of water upon waking. After dressing, meditating and preparing for your day, drink lemon water. I often have hot lemon water instead of coffee. Much more cleansing, refreshing and hydrating.

HOW MUCH SUGAR DO I NEED?

The World Health Organization recommends six teaspoons or less of added sugar a day. This is lower than the previous touted, "keep it under 10% of calorie consumption." I also adhere to having six teaspoons or less added sugar a day (over 80% of the time). This is easy to do if you are making your own meals with whole foods. Whole foods can be very convenient. One of my favorite snacks is walnuts and red berries. Yum! There are four grams of sugar in a teaspoon, so aiming at less than 24 grams is a great target. It's not hard to hit these six teaspoons or less a day if you are eating whole foods. However, it gets tough with prepackaged foods, even those marketed as being healthy. My clients become detectives and know to read the ingredients and information on the back, not just the fancy marketing on the front. Here are some label basics:

Understanding processed food. It's possible to get convenience and low process when it comes to nutrition. Some foods are more nutritionally processed! Whoa, what? The key is understanding the lingo in food processing. Anytime you cook, freeze, can, bake, or change the composition of a food, it is said to be processed. The order I like to get my food is farmer market fresh, locally grown at a grocery store, frozen, and that is it. No canned veggies. If I can't get them fresh or frozen, I will wait until they are in season. I will purchase canned fish, like tuna, on occasion but again, buy fresh or frozen. When buying nuts, get the least processed as possible, which means just the nuts, not honey roasted, dusted with chocolate, or salt.

Milk, juice, and cheese fall into the moderately processed foods category. I don't personally drink milk or juice, but my children do, and I buy the best I can find, grass-fed milk and 100% pure juice. I prefer goat's cheese but will occasionally eat other cheeses, and again, I try to find and buy the highest quality varieties I can.

Ready to eat foods like crackers, deli meats, and yogurts with fruit and fillings should be rare treats and eaten with discernment. Again, buying the highest quality with the least number of additives, including dyes, sugars, fillers, and preservatives, will keep the nutrition high.

I also watch out for low-fat items. My rule of thumb is to have the fat from real food minimally processed. That means I use real butter with no added dyes, food coloring, or salt. My favorite brand is Kerry Gold. I will also use clarified butter when cooking on a high heat at home. Most low-fat food items that are moderately and highly processed have too much added sugar. Check those yogurt labels and protein bars. I understand the need for convenience, just understand what you are choosing to nourish yourself with so you can make good choices.

Warning: Some foods that appear to be "whole," like chicken, meats, and fish, can actually have fillers and dyes added to them to keep them looking "fresh" on the store shelves. READ THE LABEL! My favorite place to get fish and other seafood is from Vital Choice. I also source chicken, beef, lamb, and pork from local farms as often as I can. A great resource to find local sources of food is a site called EATWILD.com.

While recovering from the autoimmune disorder, I sourced all my food and wouldn't touch a thing with any filler. I ate only grass-fed animals, which meant not feeding on any grain. I can't say it was convenient at the time, but neither was taking a grocery bag full of medication or having my body parts surgically removed. It actually was nicer to go to a farm, meet a farmer, check out the feed and field, and make my own informed choice. I do not have to be this dedicated now that my body is healed, I can and do eat around the 80/20 rule. Most of the time, I am eating well. You can too. Bon Appetit!

Going on an elimination diet is the best way to understand how the food you eat is tolerated by you personally. The idea is to remove potentially offending foods and slowly add them back in while monitoring a wide variety of symptoms. There are varying degrees of an elimination diet, from limiting one ingredient or food to whole food groups to the most extreme of only eating a select few foods. I followed the most restrictive elimination diet when trying to heal my body from ulcerative colitis. The duration varies from one to two weeks to months. It can take days after consuming one particular food or ingredient before your body shares how it serves you. It is important to be under the care of a nutritionist or other health care professional when undertaking an elimination diet.

ELIMINATE TOXIC SUBSTANCES AND PEOPLE

In the third pillar of the natural healing process, the first thing we have to figure out is: What is food? I don't need to convince you that prepackaged, highly preservative-laden items aren't nourishing for your body. They're really toxic. It's the kind of food you shouldn't be consuming.

These toxic substances aren't recognized by your body, and it doesn't know what to do with them, and it's very hard on your liver. Your liver is vital for nourishing your body. If you constantly provide things that your body doesn't recognize and can't use, it's very difficult for your liver. When your liver doesn't function accordingly, it will affect your entire system.

So, we need to be nice to our liver and provide real food our body can recognize and use. Before I ate lots of organic and healthy foods, I followed different diets and recommendations, and I realized it wasn't beneficial for my body. So, I had to figure out what was nourishing for me. I started an in-depth search for foods that my body could handle and were nourishing.

WHICH FOODS ARE RIGHT FOR YOU

It is very important to your health and happiness for you to understand which foods are nourishing for you. You can't just follow the latest diet advice you find on the internet or in magazines without thinking about your body's willingness and ability to use the food.

Often, when your body is trying to repair from either trauma or illness, or upset, it cannot tolerate some foods and/or ingredients that it may otherwise in less inflamed state. Emotional pain needs to be addressed along with any other aches and pains first (see Pillar #1).

For example, when I had ulcerative colitis, my body did not have the gut flora and resources to break down dairy, meat, raw vegetables as well as other food. It certainly could not tolerate nonfood items found in most diets and in the typical American diet. Now that I am healed, I can have good raw organic veggies again and anything else I choose to nourish myself with.

You have to consider first what kind of foods work for you. It is also important to keep in mind that when your body is already in a diseased state that certain foods won't be nourishing because your body cannot break down or absorb the nutrients. Being sick also means you may require more protein or not eating raw vegetables or other usually "healthy" habits.

I had to figure out which foods were good for me, and they weren't necessarily what everybody was pushing. I ate organic, healthy, natural food, and I still got sick. So, I needed to figure out which foods my body could use for nourishment and which foods I needed to leave alone. This is the same thing that you can do too.

One of the most important things that I discovered in nourishing my body with proper food is what to eat and when and what to eat together. Some foods don't combine very well for me and set up indigestion, heartburn or just food not moving nicely through the digestive tract. When food isn't broken down properly, it produces a lot of gastric diseases and symptoms because it sits in your intestines.

Your body is meant to break down the food that you provide it for nourishment and release the rest as waste. So, I'm going to share some simple food combining tips you can start utilizing in your daily eating to help move food through your digestive tract.

First is eliminating all preservatives and artificial ingredients, introducing to your system one type of food at a time. You can start with fruit. I discovered that some fruit my body handled very easily, some it didn't. The same thing could happen to you because not all of us have the same active digestive enzymes and gut flora. I had no idea that my body could not accommodate bananas. I didn't know that bananas were not nourishing for me when my body was struggling with a digestive disorder. When I started to pay attention to how I felt after eating, to my energy, my mood, and gastric symptoms, I noticed what foods were not easily digested and cut them out until I healed.

Have fruit for breakfast because it's very easy for your system to digest. Your liver is detoxing your body from about midnight to noon the next day. One of the most beneficial things that you can do for your nourishment and to rid your body of toxins is to make it easy for your digestive system in the morning.

So, fruit for breakfast. If you want melons like cantaloupe, watermelon, or honeydew, eat melons alone or leave them alone. You don't have to just have fruit for five hours, like an apple for five hours. You can have an apple and wait about an hour and have another type of fruit. That's usually how I like to do it.

Some people have a smoothie in the morning, and they combine different fruits together. I will warn you though to just pay attention first to having the fruit by itself before combining a whole bunch. Because if you combine a whole bunch of fruits and your body doesn't have a good reaction, you're not going to know which fruit it was, or maybe it was just the combination.

For my mid-day meal, I usually have protein and vegetables. So, the second thing you can do is to start implementing protein into your mid-day meal.

For my evening meal, that's the perfect time, if you're eating grains, to implement grains into your diet. Having rice in the evening will help you feel satisfied and whole. Also, it will help you sleep better. So again, implement an eating pattern your body can handle depending on your current level of health. Experiment, take notes.

As you start to implement foods back into your diet after eliminating them for a while for at least 5 to seven days, start noticing how the different foods make you feel. It's helpful to keep a log of what you're eating and how your body's reacting.

So how do you know that your body is benefiting from what you're feeding it? If you eat something and you don't feel good afterward, if your energy isn't restored and you feel lazy, tired, or irritable then that food wasn't the right food for you.

Your body should be able to easily break down the foods you put in your system. You should feel vitalized, your energy should be restored, and you should be ready to go. You don't have to give up every tiny food as I did but I highly encourage you to go on an elimination diet and pay attention to how your body reacts when you introduce a food or food combination like spaghetti with red sauce and meatballs.

Most of you are not experiencing an autoimmune disorder but can still use a cleanup in your diet for overall improvement of well-being. Going back to pillar one is also critical when thinking about making changes to your eating plan. It is beneficial to think in terms of *deserving* the best nutrients for you, how the food you are eating is serving your nutritional needs and checking in with yourself on how you feel after eating. You can use pillar two to help you breathe through your nourishment. Putting the fork down, and slowing down while eating is a great way for allowing your body to get the most from the nourishing meal you are partaking in.

NOURISHING OUR MINDS

In my work with my clients, I see a lot of anxiety, depression, and dissatisfaction with life. While addressing the nourish pillar, I explore how my client nourishes their mind and emotional or spiritual well-being. It was clear to me that high exposure to the news and social media was not nourishing!

"The way that news is presented and the way that we access news has changed significantly over the last 15 to 20 years," Graham Davey, a professor emeritus of psychology at Sussex University in the UK and editor-in-chief of the Journal of Experimental Psychopathology, told Time. "These changes have often been detrimental to general mental health."

CONCLUSION

> *"Nourish*
> *Your idea, water it, feed it, tend to it...truly nourish it*
> *or it dies! Same for your body, relationships, roses in the*
> *garden or the cucumbers."*
> - Stephanie McCannon

The third pillar of well-being, Nourish, is important to your physical, mental, and emotional well-being. We nourish our bodies to nourish our lives. If we don't have a healthy physical body, mostly attributed to lifestyle and choices we deliberately engage in, we do not have the means to enjoy our physical world. What is most important to remember is that your nourishment is your choice. Think of food in terms of appreciation instead of deprivation. Nourishment of mind and body are vital to being a happy, healthy human. What are the best choices you can make? It is not about the deprivation of mind or body. It is about INCLUSION. What am I providing for nourishment that says, "I am worthy of health and vitality"?

If you continue to think in terms of "nourishment," you will easily gravitate toward those items that are nourishing. Sometimes it is a salad...sometimes it is a shared piece of cheesecake with your friend or a birthday cake with your child. Nourishment is the key....not counting calories. If the majority of the time you are choosing to nourish your body, mind and spirit, then you can more easily handle more offending agents. This is the 80/20 rule.

Your internal guidance systems *know* what is most nourishing. Different times in our lives call for different nourishment. The more mindful, aware, and allowing of your TRUE SELF, the easier it becomes to nourish your body, mind, and soul.

The whole idea of figuring out what foods are beneficial for your body is to provide nutrients your system needs and can use right now. As you're dealing with sickness, stress, or a lack of energy and vitality, nourishing your body is key. Also, providing the right foods for right now allows your digestive system to rest, which leads us into the final pillar.

The Four Pillars of Natural Healing work together. It is not going to be enough to change your diet if other important areas of health are still poor. Many natural healing books focus solely on a diet change. It is more beneficial to focus on an eating plan that is nourishing and not a restrictive "diet." Even the word diet for most evokes a negative association to deprivation and resistance. However, it is true that when you have the other three pillars in place, you can actually get away with a more diverse diet and one that is not restrictive. I eat everything! And eventually, you will too. I especially like having carbs with an end of the day meal as I sleep better.

Action Step: What are one or two things you can do to implement what you learned? What obstacles can get in your way? How will you overcome them?

CHAPTER 6

PILLAR IV: REST

> *"Rest is not idleness, and to lie sometimes on the grass under trees on a summer's day, listening to the murmur of the water, or watching the clouds float across the sky, is by no means a waste of time."*
> - John Lubbock

According to the CDC, at least 35% of Americans don't get enough sleep, and the lack of sleep costs us over $400 billion each year. So far you have been introduced to three pillars: thinking, breathing and nourishment. It's time to learn the fourth pillar of the BolsterUP method, REST.

Rest is so vital to your health and happiness, but often shoved aside, neglected and often thought of as a waste. In fact many in Western society view resting as weak, lazy, unproductive and useless. "I'll rest when I'm dead" has often been used to poo poo the idea of being still, turning the TV off, or putting down the phone. According to research, "dead rest" will come sooner than later without adequate sleep! Sleep in fact has been shown to be more important than exercise in terms of being a happy healthy human. In fact just altering your sleep by one hour can cause death. Losing just an hour of sleep stresses the cardiovascular system, which can tip some folks with heart issues over the edge. That's why the number of heart attacks tick up significantly the day after we set the clocks ahead for daylight savings.

You need an adequate sleep and rest routine for maximum health and happiness. It is just as important to let your ideas, relationships, gardens, and mind rest. Most of the focus in this chapter, as has been in the book, is on you...Your rest, relaxation and sleep.

You've already learned three very good things to help your body rest and get adequate sleep. You are thinking positive thoughts when you go to sleep so you fall asleep easier and stay asleep. You're not up all night "worrying." You're feeling really good, relaxed, happy, and satisfied. Your body is breathing properly. You are doing the 4-7-8 breathing that's helping your body get into that relaxed state. You're nourishing your system to optimize functioning and healing. Let's step outside of ourselves and look at the environment.

One of the aspects of proper rest for your body is the environment. Your bedroom should be clean, cool, and dark. A bedroom should be one of the most welcoming, restful, and cleanest rooms in your home. If it's not, you've got a little work to do. It should also be electronics free! If you're used to having a cellphone or electronics like a TV in your room, you should turn them off, especially if you have trouble sleeping and staying asleep at night. If you keep your phone on Wi-Fi mode or if you have a lot of electrical impulses running around your room, it can definitely disrupt your sleep cycle.

If you use your phone for an alarm, that's fine. Just turn off the Wi-Fi and place it in "sleep mode" before you go to sleep so you won't be bothered to check statuses and other things on the internet. Even if you are not checking all the updates on your phone, the Wi-Fi itself can be disruptive to your sleep cycle. This should be a no-brainer. Keep your electronics out of your resting room. That will help you tremendously. If you have a TV and you can't get rid of it, close it behind a cabinet. Open it when you're viewing it and close it if you're not.

When you're sleeping or resting, that's when your body's going into deep repair mode. Resting is the only time your body is able to fully relax and repair itself. Ideally, you should be getting about eight hours of sleep a night. More sleep and rest are essential if you are ill. Your body's too busy when you're up walking around throughout the day. It's thinking and digesting and having a good time. It's also working, doing things, and serving and being served. It's not really healing or repairing itself if it's in a busy state.

Sleeping is vital for your health, happiness, as a human. If inanimate objects need to rest, reboot, or shut down, then more so for you as a biological being. It is just as much a priority as water, and food. Rest is very critical and it makes a huge difference to your feelings as far as your happiness. How many of you are exhausted and just don't feel like responding very nicely to people if they're asking you questions? We snap at them. When I'm tired, that's the time I'm most likely to say something that I don't really like, to my children particularly, that I don't necessarily want to convey. But I'm tired, and I'm not operating at my best. So resting is vital to your happiness and your health, and how you behave and interact as a human.

All animals inherently know if they are sick or injured to lay down. Many will find a stream of water to lay by and stay there for days until they are healed. However, most humans do not exercise the same practice. If we are sick or injured, many of us push ourselves to go work, do the laundry, or stay in the game! When we adopt the practice of the wild…be still if we are sick or injured, we assist healing. Rest is crucial for healing. This is true for physical, mental and emotional healing.

Not getting the recommended 7 to 9 hours of sleep has a tremendous impact on your life experience. Being sleep-deprived decreases your problem-solving ability, reaction time, and communication. We are not able to concentrate, focus or learn. In addition, our irritability leads to reacting instead of responding to others. Moodiness and loss of productivity are not the only determinants to sleep deprivation. Our health suffers too. A lack of adequate rest can kill you. That's scary, but thankfully, I can share with you how you can start getting adequate rest and live a healthy, happy life. Developing good sleep hygiene can change your life dramatically.

REAL LIFE STORY

> *"We humans have lost the wisdom of genuinely resting and relaxing. We worry too much.*
> *We don't allow our bodies to heal, and we don't allow our minds and hearts to heal."*
> **- Thich Nhat Hanh**

It is no secret that getting enough sleep for your individual needs is vital to health and essential to healing and happiness. It is very difficult to just stop everything in our life if we find our bodies struggling with sickness or disease. Most of society looks unfavorably at taking time off for a sabbatical or enough time off to allow for true healing. However, depending on your level of stress or disease, resting is exactly what your body needs.

Of course, this requires you to make some lifestyle choices. Although at first, you may believe you can't take time off from work, you truly can't afford not to. Health is wealth. Eventually, if you don't take the necessary rest your body is demanding, then you won't be here at all.

I had to make a very difficult decision that affected my whole family, many people that relied on me, and my community. As we know, stress is a major contributor to our health and well-being. I was suffering from an autoimmune disorder and realized I needed to rest or die. Our mental state and outlook, as well as our ability to process and respond appropriately to the challenges in our day is affected by our sleep. After much thought and consideration, I made the decision to shut down my manufacturing business and give the gift of rest to my body, and the gift of life to my children. I needed more sleep, and the only way I was going to get it was to decrease the demands of my day at the time. I had 3 young children and was completely on my own to raise them and provide for all their daily needs. It was either my kids or my business… I was doing my business for my family! So if I was going to rest, the demands of my business needed to go.

I'm not telling you to quit your job. However, you must fully take into account the physical and mental demands you place on your body. I dedicated myself to a good sleep hygiene habit and radically improved my health and happiness.

What can you do to provide more opportunities for resting for your body?

Sleep is the ultimate rest, and it's not just how but when. However, throughout your day, you can take "resting breaks." One of the things you can do to provide more rest without fully going to sleep is to close your eyes in a quiet setting and concentrate on your breathing for a few minutes. Just two to three minutes of rest throughout your day is highly beneficial.

DETAILED SCIENTIFIC EVIDENCE

If you sleep less than six hours a night and have disturbed sleep, you stand a 48 % greater chance of developing or dying from heart disease. In addition, not getting enough sleep can result in weight gain. Our mental health suffers and lack of sleep has been linked to depression, mood disorders, and dementia.

Research shows that sleep deprivation is essentially the same as binge-drinking, as in, you literally become cognitively impaired. Improper sleep, or sleep deprivation, has an enormous impact on your well-being. Matt Walker, professor of neuroscience and psychology at the University of California, Berkeley, and author of *Why We Sleep*, concludes sleep either restores our health or destroys it. He is also the founder and director of the Center for Human Sleep Science. Sleep deprivation has a tremendous effect on our health, happiness, and humanity. It affects learning in children (and adults), productivity, mood, disease, and can shorten life expectancy.

Dr. Walker says there are sufficient and casual links to diseases that are destroying life, from diabetes, heart disease, and cancer to depression and suicide. Sleep, good proper sleep, is essential to normal biological functioning. The end result is short sleep or resting cycles equals a short life or premature death.

Not getting enough quality rest creates a toxic protein load called beta-amyloid. In addition, his research has shown the lack of sleep weakens your immune system, making you more susceptible to disease and less likely to control or heal when you do get sick. Improper sleep hygiene also encourages overeating. *Sleep is more important than exercise* according to sleep doctor experts like Dr. Walker. Yes, that is right. It is more important than working out, which is more stress for an already exhausted body.

Dr. Walker also warns against sleeping pills, referring to them as "bad." Just like alcohol, sleeping pills do not produce naturalistic sleep, they knock you out. Sedation is not sleep. Approximately 10 million people take some sleep aid every month and the numbers rise as we get older. Sleeping pills "do not provide natural sleep, can damage health, and increase the risk of life-threatening diseases." What's more alarming is they are to be used for short term only, and actually increase insomnia when use is halted. This sounds pretty terrifying. Let's look at alcohol and sleep.

Three issues with alcohol and sleep. First, alcohol shuts down your cortex as a sedative, and you are not actually sleeping. Secondly, your sleep is interrupted many more times, although you may not be aware of the disruption. This may be why the feeling of being restored is elusive upon waking after a night of drinking or even a nightcap. Third, alcohol blocks dream sleep or the rapid eye movement (REM) sleep state. REM sleep is tied to good emotional and mental health. A 1980's study denied rats of REM sleep and found they died at the same rate as being deprived of food. Dream sleep is vital to our health, happiness, and humanity. Marijuana also blocks REM sleep and should be avoided as a sleep aid as well.

Teenagers are considered high risk for lack of sleep, with less than 3% getting recommended 9 hours of sleep. The natural sleep cycle of a teen is more in line with what Dr. Brewers calls the wolf, or commonly referred to as a night owl. Teens' natural hormonal cycle wakes them up around 10 AM, and they become more productive later in the day and naturally want to sleep after 11 PM. Early rise times for schools that start at 7:30 or even 8:00 are horribly detrimental to teens.

For more than a decade, dedicated research and scientists have been isolating sleep and immunological memory. In other words, sleep cycles and the regulation of immune function and our capacity to heal. These studies look at T cells, pro-inflammatory cytokines, and inflammation. The conclusion is that sleep enhances immune function, defense mechanisms, and results in healing.[3]

---

[3] (Besedovsky, L., Lange, T., & Born, J. (2012). Sleep and immune function. *Pflugers Archiv : European journal of physiology, 463*(1), 121–137. https://doi. org/10.1007/s00424-011-1044-0)

Other sleep and behavior experts rely on other forms of treatment not associated with drugs. American College of Physicians, or ACP — officially endorsed what many meta-analyses have found: Cognitive behavioral therapy for insomnia, or CBT-I, is the best treatment for chronic insomnia disorder and should be the first line of treatment for the approximately 24 million adults suffering from the condition. The behavior therapy includes sleep restriction, belief and thought associations about sleep, and good sleep hygiene. However, CBT-I can take days to weeks to see improvement and most folks would rather take a pill. Although as research shows there is no short cut, and actually no sleep either.

In addition to the above scientific research, Dr. Michael Breus, renowned sleep doctor and author of *The Power of When*, established four different natural chronotypes to help use a deeper, and more influential approach to CBT-I. Each chronotype dictates your best sleep patterns, times of day to be optional, as well as how to best participate in your day-to-day activities all to garner the best rest for you. Not only does Dr. Breus uncover the reason for difficulty in engaging in modern lifestyles and demands for each chronotype, but he provides workable solutions that aid in the individual's overall well-being. Just understanding there is a natural divergence in each individual's sleep patterns has provided me with more grace, understanding, and willingness to allow others to be true to themselves, during the waking and sleeping hours.

He describes four chronotypes and when each gets the best sleep as well as functions optimally through the day. The categories of chronotypes are linked to animals found in the wild: Dolphin, Lion, Bear, and Wolf.

It's no secret that many of us are aware that we are more alert early in the morning or come alive at night. However, given the structure of our current society, those that are most alert later in the day, or what I grew up referring to as "night owls," can often be perceived as lazy.

The explanation, according to Dr. Breus and his research, is due to chronotypes. Night owls or "wolves" are often diagnosed with insomnia. Often, the Wolf chronotype is foggy-headed and has difficulty concentrating for much of the "day." Those that seek medical treatment (not sleep doctors) end up on sleeping pills, antidepressants, and antipsychotic medications, according to Dr. Breus. When really, it is their natural rhythm to be up during the night. However, this pushes against the 9-5 clock and produces a lack of productivity at work and poor quality of life for the individual. In fact, Dr. Breus highlights a patient about to be fired due to being a "wolf" in a "bear" world.

Let's briefly go through the four chronotypes. If you are interested in finding out what your chronotype is, there is a link in the reference section to the quiz.

Dolphins account for around 10% of the population. As unihemispheric sleepers, they always have one side of their brain alert, ready to rouse the troops when needed. Dolphins are often seen as intelligent and neurotic.

Kind of cool. But each chronotype has its ups and downs. Dolphins as well as Lions and Wolves, fall outside what we consider to be normal sleep/wake patterns in today's society. This can wreak havoc on their professional and personal lives. Understanding your type and Dr. Breus' suggestions for integrating your chronotype into everyday living can mean the difference from mere existence to living as a happy, healthy human.

Lions (I happen to be one) are morning people. Often awake without an alarm right before the sun comes up. Lions are most active, alert, and creative earlier in the day. However, don't expect them to make it through the evening news. Lions tend to be optimistic and account for about 15 to 20% of the population.

Bears make up the bulk of society, at least 50%, and match the patterns of 9-5 workweeks. They are easy-going, snackers, sleep at the drop of a hat, outgoing, friendly, and fit well into daylight hours.

Wolves you have been introduced to, and I find them to be the most intriguing, most likely because they are a direct opposite to me (lion). Wolves are nocturnal, have a high creative extrovert personality, and like Lions, make up about 15-20%

of the population. Dr. Brues' explanation for this is tribal. In order to foster a thriving population, guards needed to be on call 24/7.

If you asked a Lion to stay up all night when they are naturally sleepy at nightfall, the whole village could be wiped out by predators or enemies. However, a Wolf would be fully alert, engaged, and ready for anything that threatened the livelihood of the people. The same is true in reverse.

What I find so eloquent about Dr. Brues' studies and the four chronotypes is it alleviates unworthiness felt by so many who feel like a round peg being shoved in a square hole.

Neurotic people are considered one of the "Big Five" personality traits (the others are extroversion, agreeableness, conscientiousness, and openness to experience). Dolphins are beautiful, sought-after creatures in the wild, and the same is true for all the chronotypes. My point is, in terms of being a happy, healthy human, it's important to know as much about yourself as possible and how to best move forward to enjoy the most satisfaction from life. If you discover you are a true Wolf, find a way to work at night. Lions, know you need to get your most important meetings and work done early in the day. Bears, be conscious of breaks and downtime, and Dolphins, be aware of your energy throughout the day.

Let's address a new phenomenon many of us may be engaged in, especially with a hectic daytime demanding work life.

Revenge Bedtime Procrastination (RBP). This term comes from a study done in 2014 in the Netherlands. RBP is refusal to shut your eyes when you know you should, and yes, it is an actual psychological phenomenon. It boils down to a control issue and fear of missing out. You don't feel like you have much choice in your day, or get to participate in "you" time, so you deliberately refuse to go to bed until a later hour. Honor yourself and your physical, mental, and emotional needs for sleep.

REAL LIFE STORY

Just as my thinking, breathing, and nourishment were playing key roles in my health, happiness, and well-being, so was my rest. During the height of my disease, I was not sleeping much and certainly did not understand the need to rest, to take breaks, vacations, time out for my self-care, or time away from work. If I wasn't busy or moving, then I felt I wasn't productive. This is a very Western or American thought process. It is ingrained in us that doing nothing is wrong or lazy. However, in other areas of the world, resting, taking time off, and tending to self-care are just as important to the workday as the actual work. Rest was another shift I needed to understand and participate in for my health, happiness, and overall well-being.

I do make the distinction between rest and sleep. We can rest with our eyes closed like during meditation but not be sleeping. Sleeping is vital for our health, and many experts are now hailing the benefits or detriments of not having adequate quality and quantity for our well-being. When I started applying proper sleep to my regime along with thinking, breathing and nourishment, my health dramatically improved.

Dr. Matt Walker points out the deadly results of losing just one hour of sleep. Every year, daylight savings times force the loss of one hour of sleep and clocks shift forward. Heart attacks, fatal car accidents, and strokes all spike each and every year during this shift. I myself ran into a ditch in my early twenties after working a late night shift. Remember I am a lion, and night time is NOT my best time. It's extremely difficult for me to stay alert the later the evening gets.

Start School Later is an advocacy group promoting student health and education by raising public awareness about the correlation between sleep and school hours. By starting school just one hour later, there has been a decrease in the number of suicides, car accidents, and sports injuries. As a home and hospital teacher I used this to my advantage. I would deliberately schedule any high school students for no earlier than 10:00 AM. Parents thought I was some kind of miracle worker as their children's test scores and "attention" miraculously improved. I was also very liked as a teacher, more because I thought of my students as a whole person not just a student.

PRACTICE TO APPLY NOW

BEDTIME THINKING

This technique will set your body and mind up for the best night's sleep. I started practicing this over a dozen years ago, and I still do it every morning and evening. It's very important to set your body up in a positive, relaxed, and happy state before it goes into its healing cycle. The healing cycle is when you're sleeping. Your body voluntarily heals when you are in a calm state and sleeping is your best calm state.

When you're about to lay your head on the pillow, that is not the time to be going through your day, recounting all the things that you didn't particularly care for. It is not the time to start focusing on hurt or sadness or not feeling good. You're going to use your mind, to deliberately focus on what you want... better health, better relationships, more abundance and the feelings of having what you want. You're going to use it to help heal your body and to maintain health, and happiness.

So, as you're laying with your head on the pillow, I want you to start thinking of thoughts that make you feel good, really good. Things that are positive. They can be from a past experience; they can even be from when you were a child. It can be a future event that you are really looking forward to that makes you feel good.

The idea is to create a feeling, through what you are thinking, of satisfaction and contentment. You want your body to feel relaxed, happy, and satisfied, so you have to think of satisfying things. It does not necessarily have to be tied to health. Not at all. You know, often, I'm thinking of a really fun time that I had with a family member or a friend. Sometimes I think about something that I received that I really wanted. That makes me feel good, and I go to sleep with a smile on my face and happiness in my heart, and I want you to as well. My body is then relaxed, so will yours.

You can also repeat to yourself, "I am a well-being. I am whole."

That's what I want you to start doing as you lay your head on the pillow or when you relax on your couch. Yes, you may have to really try hard to think about some positive things in your life, but I know that you can do it. I know you can!

The next thing that I want you to do before you ever get up out of bed in the morning is to repeat that process. Before your feet even hit the floor, you've got to start focusing on feeling good, feeling great. Feel good and believe that the day is going to be another great day and things are going to go your way.

If you have events that you know are coming up in your day, I want you to visualize them going your way. For example, if that day, you are going to have a meeting, visualize that it's going to be successful. See your co-workers high-fiving you or your boss shaking your hand. If you have phone calls that you have to make, visualize the other person picking up the phone and agreeing with everything that you have to say. Start to visualize your day going your way. Before you get out of bed, make sure that you've gained that happy, peaceful, and satisfied feeling. Sometimes I have to lay there a bit. Occasionally, when my kids get me out of bed before I want to get out of bed, I go back to bed and do it right! I want to start my day on the best foot, and to start my day with positive thinking.

ENVIRONMENT

Your bedroom is for two things only. Sleep is one and I am guessing you can figure out the other. No exercise equipment, office supplies, or stacks of laundry belong in your resting nest. One of the aspects of proper rest for your body is the environment. The room temperature and amount of light are also important to good sleep hygiene. I know for sure I sleep best in a cool, dark room with just the right amount of weight for blankets. Ideally, room temperature should be between 65 to 67 degrees Fahrenheit. We are biological beings. The absence of light creates hormonal shifts, like melatonin, that tell the body it's time for sleep. The need for darkness for a good night's sleep is another reason to not have the TV on before trying to fall asleep. Set your thermostat to automatically cool down to 65 degrees at your normal bedtime. I set mine to cool down starting at 9 PM for my usual bedtime of ten.

I also recommend a weighted blanket. Weighted blankets have been used for those that suffer from anxiety to autism. I feel more comfortable sleeping with weight on me. I used to achieve this with about 7 different blankets and quilts! Just be mindful of the heaviness. Heavier is not better. My current weighted blanket is 15 pounds. I have been under a 30-pound blanket that felt like cement. It was not comfortable for me at all. Now that we have an idea of blankets, let's get the best sheets possible. And no, it's not about thread count.

WHAT ARE YOU SLEEPING ON?

Believe it or not, the type of sheets you are sleeping on will benefit your body and aid in healing, and sleep.

What are you sleeping on? The most beneficial material to sleep on is linen. Linen has historically been touted as the best and most beneficial fabric. I started practicing this after being diagnosed with my autoimmune disorder. Flax as a seed is highly nutritious, and the benefits continue when the stalks are made into fabric. Linen sheets (all 100% linen fabric) are bacteria resistant, breathable, have a natural PH balance, and are moisture absorbing with evaporating capabilities, making them ideal for anyone with skin irritations, in addition to the world's best bedding. It is one of if not the oldest known fabrics. Royalty was dressed in it, and Pharaohs wrapped in it. Plus, linen is twice as durable as cotton. Just make sure you are getting the real thing. It transformed my sleeping habits. Linen is a healing fabric, some say, and if nothing else, a sweet luxury that you are worth. If you are going to spend a third of your life doing something, shouldn't it be on the best possible fabric? Since your body is doing the most healing while it's sleeping, it's just an added bonus to be sleeping on linen sheets. Linen is such a wonderful fabric to begin with.

Hands down, it is the best material for restful sleep. It has hypoallergenic properties and feels good. I'm not talking about that scratchy raw linen. I'm talking about really nice linen sheets. Allowing your body to sleep in one of the best fabrics available to us will result in a healthier sleep cycle. Linen is environmentally friendly. It can speed up the recovery process and allow your body to maintain health. Who knew linen was so great for your health and happiness?

You can find linen sheets at places like Restoration Hardware. There are lots of linen sheets online that you can start pursuing. Now I know good linen sheets can cost a bit. I offer you two solutions. The first is to make it a priority to have linen sheets! When we prioritize things in life, they have a way of working out. Tell family and friends that is what you want for a gift, or let them know you are saving up for them. When you have put enough money aside, buy them. Just be mindful that you're getting quality 100% linen, not a blend. After all... all "bedding and towels" are called "linens" now. The folks at www. bedthread.com have good tests for true linen bedding.

The second solution is to make your own. My first set of linen sheets, I sewed them myself. I bought a bolt of linen. I have a king-size bed, so I had to sew two big pieces together for it to work. I still have those linen sheets after over ten years! My whole household sleeps on linen sheets. My children sleep on linen; I sleep on linen. My guests sleep on linen. Just make it a priority. Linen is life! I even wrap myself in linen when I meditate sometimes.

REST CONCLUSION

> *"Sleep is the best meditation."*
> **- Dalai Lama**

Adequate sleep affects every area of your life from your physical health and appearance to your mental state and mood. These are good healthy habits to get into to allow your body to rest and repair at night. To ensure a restful night's sleep, make sure Wi-Fi is off, electronics are off and out of sight (ideally two hours before you go to bed), your room is inviting and clean, dark and cool. Good sleep hygiene involves time, temperature, and temperament. You can even slip into your favorite linen pajamas. I take linen pj's with me when I sleep outside my own linen dressed bed.

The aspect of time for good sleep hygiene includes the number of hours as well as consistency of going to bed around the same hour. As Dr. Walker's, Dr. Brewer's and other sleep scientist research suggests, it is imperative to your health and happiness to get at least six hours of quality sleep, no less. You can find an appropriate time to get to bed by utilizing the Power of When suggestions for your chronotype by taking the Power of When quiz.

> *"Sleep is the golden chain that ties health and our bodies together."*
> - Thomas Dekker

In addition, your bedtime thinking, breathing, and how you nourished yourself will impact your sleep cycle. Sleep is not a luxury or something to put off when you have nothing else to do. It is a pillar of health, happiness and humanity.

Action Step: What are one or two things you can do to implement what you learned? What obstacles can get in your way? How will you overcome them?

EXERCISE VERSUS MOVEMENT

I am including this chapter on exercise because it was key to my own healing. What I am about to share with you goes against most popular advice in regard to stress and health. Here it goes: You need to exercise less. Yes, that is right. Prolonged cardio workouts that many of us have bought into as "exercise" are not good for you. There are two key issues with exercise I want to discuss with you. One is what you might consider exercise, and the other is how long and often you should be exercising.

While exercise, of course, involves movement, movement in and of itself is not exercise.

True exercise is a stress on your physical body. Before I go too far into this, let's define exercise and movement.

Exercise needs to take into consideration the duration, frequency, intensity, and mode. How long, often, and hard are you participating in a given activity? True exercise is supposed to include a substantial physical effort to create change and improve health and fitness.

Perhaps, like me, you were under the impression that to "exercise," it meant jogging or running for thirty minutes to an hour. Or perhaps make sure you are in some cardio class at least three days a week. For many, the mindset that exercise needs to be prolonged for thirty minutes at least in order to be effective is incorrect and can be dangerous.

The notion of exercise involving a sustained cardiac output for a long period is outdated and harmful. Running or bouncing around a cardio room for half an hour or more is very stressful to your system. If you are already experiencing high levels of stress that your body is reacting to, trying to keep your heart rate up for too long is more harmful than beneficial.

Now, I am not telling you not to exercise. What I am asking is that you think about exercise in a way you may not have. Exercise specialist Dr. McGuff, who wrote *Body by Science,* has changed my life. He goes into great length, discussing the error of prolonged cardio workouts for exercise and health.

Dr. McGuff and many others have come to the conclusion that brief, intense functional movement, like sprinting or lifting really heavy weights, or lifting weights very, very slowly while maintaining relaxed breathing for a few minutes a week is all you need.

For some of you, this is the key to your healing and maintaining health as well as decreasing the effects of stress on your body. What you think you are doing for the good of your body could, in fact, be what is tearing you down instead of building you up.

I had a very difficult time grasping that my hour-long runs and one-hour cardio class were responsible for my intense migraines. When I stopped the prolonged cardio and started "exercising" less, my health improved, my mood improved, and my energy level stabilized.

I encourage you to check out the *Body by Science* book (Resources Section) for further instruction or find a facility near you to improve your health. Instead of hours a week, I went to twelve minutes. Yes, increasing my workload for a shorter period of time worked. Yes, just 12 minutes a week is all you need.

For some of you, the flip side is more true. You may not be getting enough exercise and engage in very little movement.

Movement is necessary to your health and well-being. Movement is just that…moving. Going for a walk, which is not considered exercising due to the lack of intensity. Walking is movement. Full out sprinting for a minute would be exercise. You should be moving throughout your day. Stretching, yoga, playing with your kids, walking up the stairs are beneficial movements for your body.

I encourage you to move more, exercise less. However, your exercise needs to be intense enough that after 12 minutes, you can't do any more. And you are not going to exercise like this every day. Once a week or every ten days or so. The rest of your week, you can walk, do yoga, gently ride a bike, etc.

Action Step: What are one or two things you can do to implement what you learned? What obstacles can get in your way? How will you overcome them?

CONCLUSION

My goal for this book was to introduce you to The Four Pillars of being a happy healthy human and how you can start *today* to implement each of them into your life for healing and happiness by self-managing your thinking, breathing, nourishment and rest. The last thought I want to leave you with is a reminder of what you've learned in this book that will help you on your path to a healthier, happier you.

We earn our disease, although we may not recognize how it happens. Stress, negative thought patterns, improper breathing, lack of nourishing foods, and poor rest all play a role in your well-being. By having The Four Pillars as part of your daily life, you can start to take back control of your life.

The key to The Four Pillars is rhythm. That's the beauty of it! If you lack in one area, the other three will hold you up. They all rely on and support each other. Just focusing on positive thoughts won't do much if your breathing is off, you have a poor diet, or you don't get adequate rest. Just as important, you can't sit around resting all the time either! Each pillar plays a unique and vital role.

All four pillars are important. One may need more of your attention than the others right now. Pay attention to what you need, and take steps toward change. The resources mentioned above are a great place to start!

The Four Pillars of being a Happy Healthy Human are available to you right here, right now. The good news is that restoring your area, or areas, of weakness will produce healing, well-being, and happiness.

It is my goal that you find your way back to health. I am certain our bodies know what to do and are, in fact, trying to be healthy and balanced. With the instructions and tools provided in this book, you can have what you seek — health and happiness. I also invite you to join the BolsterUp community and if you are looking for more guidance and support sign up for the online course at BolsterUp.com. BolsterUP is about you living a life you love full of health and vitality. Keep an eye out for retreats, and special programs offered throughout the year. I am super proud that you took the time to invest in yourself, your happiness. As you improve all of humanity improves with you.

THE END

ABOUT THE AUTHOR

As I write this, Teddy, our golden retriever, naps by me on the couch. My partner's hand is placed gently on my knee, as we share the warmth of the fire. My home is filled with chatter and laughter as my adult children are home buzzing around in the kitchen. I feel content. At peace. Happy.

But life wasn't always like this. While my life used to look perfect on the outside, I was suffering on the inside. I was in an unfulfilling marriage, filled with stress and shame, and couldn't bring myself to reach out or get help. It wasn't until

I was diagnosed with a devastating autoimmune disorder and had to face the idea that my two toddlers might grow up without a mom that I was spurred into action.

The doctors and specialists couldn't tell me how to get better and the only options they gave me were aggressive drug therapy, getting body parts removed, or simply preparing to die. But I wasn't going to give up that easily so I started my own search for health, happiness and satisfaction.

As I kept digging deeper I uncovered a mountain of research connecting stress, unhappiness, disease, and the ancient wisdom of our own bodies and neurology. I learned the power and strength that my body had and after healing I dedicated myself to helping others find their own peace, happiness and health using what I now call the BolsterUp Method.

For the past 20 years I've used these principles to help CEOs expand their business, mothers learn the value of Vitamin "P", and health care and service providers to accelerate their patients' health and happiness, as well as their own. I LOVE what I do, and thank my own journey, suffering and life lessons that have allowed me to give back so much more to those willing to BolsterUp. I'm so glad you're here!

To find out more visit StephanieMcCannon.com

RESOURCES

Body by Science, Dr. Doug McGuff, John Little, McGraw Hill Education, 2009

The Oxygen Advantage: Simple, Scientifically Proven Breathing Techniques to Help You Become Healthier, Slimmer, Faster, and Fitter, Patrick McKeown, William Morrow Paperbacks, 2016

Happy Healthy and Healed, Stephanie McCannon

Link to online resources: BolsterUpMethod.com

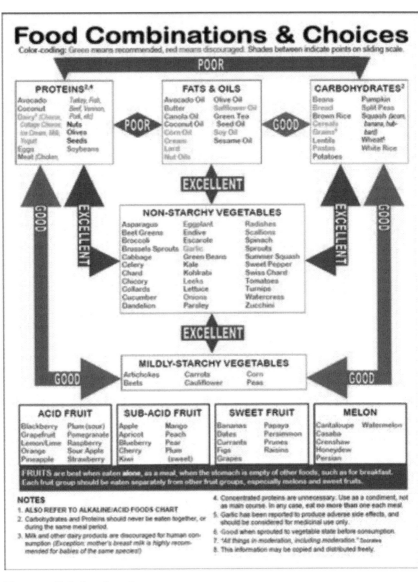

Photo credit:kaleuniversity.org

BolsterUp! Eating Plan: The Happiness Diet

1. Eat Whole Food, Mostly Plants

2. Eat whole foods that are nourishing for you right now.

3. Eat produce that is in season

4. Connect Contribute and Control

THE LINK BETWEEN FOOD AND FEELINGS

Did You Know?

Recent scientific evidence suggests that food and diet may play a role in the prevention and management of certain mental health conditions, including Depression, Anxiety, Schizophrenia, Attention Deficit Hyperactivity Disorder (ADHD) and Alzheimer's Disease.

We are walking chemical factories.

It is more important what *you don't* eat than what you do! By eliminating processed foods, too much sugar, and too much animal products you can greatly influence your overall happiness, health and wellbeing.

Certain foods are key components in the making of powerful, mood-altering chemicals in the brain. The chemicals, called neurotransmitters, not only boost your mood but improve sleep, increase pain tolerance, jog your memory and improve performance.

Serotonin: mood stabiliser, wellbeing, happiness

Oxytocin: Bonding, love, trust

Endorphins: Pain relief, runner's high, relaxation

Serotonin boosting foods:

Serotonin is a chemical messenger that's believed to act as a mood stabilizer. It's said to help produce healthy sleeping patterns as well as boost your mood. Your body changes L-tryptophan into serotonin.

1. Asparagus
2. Salmon
3. Walnuts

Oxytocin Boosting Foods:

1. Mushroom
2. Spinach
3. Avocados

Endorphin Boosting Foods:

1. Cacao (at least 72% chocolate)
2. Lemon infused water
3. Vanilla bean

Think of food in terms of energy. Lots of fresh vegetables are like clear glass. The more processed items added is like adding mud to the clean, clear glass. Even when the mud is dumped out, it leaves a residue, and you can no longer see through the glass. Our diets can either leave us feeling clean and clear like the see-through glass or sluggish and dull like the muddy glass.

THANK YOU

Thank You For Reading My Book!

I really appreciate all of your feedback, and I love hearing what you have to say. If this book has helped you at all, please leave a positive review.

If there is more information you are seeking, please contact me by email at contact@ StephanieMccannon.com.

I need your input to make the next version of this book and my future books even better.

Please leave me a helpful review on Amazon letting me know what you thought of the book.

HAPPY
SELF PUBLISHING

Happy Self Publishing is a one-stop destination for publishing services such as book cover design, editing, formatting, audiobook narration, website design, and marketing. At Happy Self Publishing we help authors find their voice and self-publish professionally.

▶ **WHAT WE DO:** We help coaches, consultants, trainers, speakers, and entrepreneurs who aspire to position themselves as the trusted experts in their field by helping them become bestselling authors within 6 months or less, even if they hate writing.

▶ **HOW WE DO IT:** We show you how to build a profitable author funnel and use the book as the lead magnet in the funnel to give you expert positioning and attract qualified leads for your business.

▶ **WHY IT WORKS:** After working with over 400 authors from 35 countries, we've been able to simplify the process and show you the easiest and fastest way to publish your book. It doesn't matter at what stage of your author journey you are currently - we have the tools & resources to take you to the next step and help you publish a world-class book.

▶ **SERVICES WE PROVIDE:**
✓ book writing aka angel writing
✓ book coaching
✓ editing
✓ book cover design
✓ formatting
✓ publishing ebooks, paperback & audiobooks
✓ global distribution
✓ author websites
✓ book trailers
✓ bestseller promotions

🌐 www.happyselfpublishing.com
✉ writetous@happyselfpublishing.com

Schedule a free Book Strategy
Call with us to discuss your book project:
www.happyselfpublishing.com/call

165

Made in the USA
Middletown, DE
09 September 2022

72741287R00109